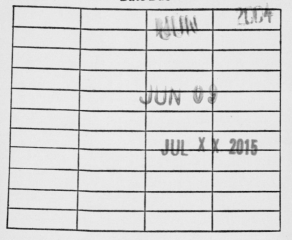
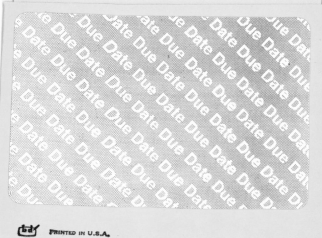

AN ANATOMY
OF
MILTON'S VERSE

An Anatomy

of

Milton's Verse

✠

by

W. B. C. WATKINS

ARCHON BOOKS

Hamden, Connecticut

1965

67-6976

LIBRARY OF CONGRESS CATALOG CARD NUMBER: 65-24505
PRINTED IN THE UNITED STATES OF AMERICA

IN MEMORY OF
DONALD STAUFFER
1902–1952

Preface

SINCE THE TURN of this century it has been commonplace to marvel that the orthodox during the preceding two hundred years accepted Milton's individual theology as uncritically as Pope overlooked the negation of Christianity in his *Essay on Man*. Can it be that they concentrated on the poetry?

In our time scholars have so ingeniously retraced the mazes of Milton's reading that he seems now to have had few thoughts or images of his own; theologians have finally untangled his heresies, astronomers his cosmology; psychiatrists and a novelist have analyzed his marital relations. Until recently poets and critics, reversing the Romantics and Victorians, have been often busy discrediting his esthetic. Milton has appeared in many guises: theologian, politician, educator, priest and prophet, case history of marital failure, perverter of language and prosody.

In this frequently brilliant and valuable speculation we were in danger of missing a central truth. Milton himself considered poetry of paramount importance in his life, and good poetry, he thought, is "simple, sensuous, passionate." [1] With all its complexities and ambiguities, to a unique extent his own poetry embodies these basic qualities. To demonstrate this is the sole purpose of these three essays.

[1] I shall not twist this phrase, out of context.

vii

I do not mean to disparage investigation of intellectual background, for ideas are certainly an essential part of Milton's poetry. As a result of fertile research, our age is better equipped to understand him than any since his own. Nor do I mean to imply that poetic values have been entirely neglected all these years. Critics like Tillyard, ignoring crosscurrents of fashion and controversy, have long been quietly at work. But until a few years ago studies of Milton were out of balance. Research was outpacing criticism. His craft and style—his whole conception of poetry—were left mainly to a hostile school very much in the public eye. Without sufficient warning young readers succumbed to "the active campaign against Milton . . . conducted by younger guerilla warriors."[2] While scholars were absorbed in fresh approaches, the public turned away.

Now the tide has begun to turn, balance to be restored. Brooks, Hardy, Stein, and Allen have already made less imperative my own intention of a direct, uncomplicated approach to Milton's poetry. Their books in some ways anticipate, in others corroborate, my own views; yet my approach cuts across as much as it parallels theirs. In this book, intended for the general reader,[3] I have tried to keep marginal comment to a minimum, in order not to be distracted from Milton by running arguments and skirmishes.

In the necessary attempt to isolate distinctive qualities of emotion and tone there is always danger of "biographical" interpretation. But poetry is neither com-

[2] Douglas Bush, *Paradise Lost in Our Time*, 6.
[3] Therefore, for convenience, all quotations from Milton are from the Cambridge Edition, revised by H. F. Fletcher.

posed nor read in a vacuum; the critic must trust what discernment and tact he has to avoid irrelevancies of personality. I am confident that the contemporary reader will not consider such words as "frustration," "conflict," "ambivalence" intended to suggest serious psychological abnormality or profound neurosis. And the casual references to James Joyce's great but obscure prose poem on Original Sin and the Fall of Man will not, I hope, needlessly distract, while serving to remind readers that Milton's themes still fascinate our most imaginative writers.

Calling this short book *An Anatomy of Milton's Verse* may arouse false expectations. I chose the older term "anatomy" partly for its seventeenth century flavor, partly as warning that what follows will be more a series of demonstrations than an analysis in the exhaustive modern fashion, and partly because "anatomy" suggests my concern with physical qualities, with instincts and senses. We know that infinite care went into Milton's most spontaneous and "unpremeditated verse," [4] just as great complexity underlies his simplicity. My own emphasis is more on the unpremeditated, the instinctive and emotional in Milton, than on his intellectual control, though intellect and emotion do not function separately in creation.

It is by examining his living poetry that we understand what Milton means to us today, which is not precisely what he meant to preceding or will mean to following generations. Poetic analysis is a dangerous and limited

---

[4] . . . my celestial patroness, who . . . inspires
Easy my unpremeditated verse . . .

P. L., IX, 21 ff.

but essential technique. Too often it turns out to be autopsy and at best is only vivisection of an immortal body. Fortunately, good poems can be wounded but never killed. Like Milton's angels, they

Cannot but by annihilating die.

There is little in the introductory chapter, "Sensation," which will be unfamiliar to all readers of Milton, yet much which many critics neglect. To establish once more his extraordinary sensuous endowment is essential to every exploration of his poetry. The second chapter, building on the first, by avoiding so far as possible Milton's theology and rationalism, attempts to demonstrate the positive and brilliant success of *Paradise Lost* and its lasting value for less theologically-minded ages than the seventeenth century. In the third chapter, "Temptation," what I have to say about *Comus* and *Paradise Regained* is controversial, but at least does not pretend to be *complete* interpretation of either poem. In using the partial failure of *Paradise Regained* to throw light on the rarity of Milton's achievement in *Paradise Lost* and *Samson Agonistes*, I may be occasionally too severe. But when all is said, *Paradise Regained* (and to a slight extent *Comus*) remains too much circumscribed by the seventeenth century to be fully recapturable in our time.

This book owes being to the Trustees of the John Simon Guggenheim Memorial Foundation, to whom I am deeply grateful.

W. B. C. Watkins

Laurel, Mississippi
May, 1955

Contents

AN ANATOMY
OF
MILTON'S VERSE

Sensation

NOTHING REVEALS more clearly that Milton's poetry is simple, sensuous, passionate than exploration of his imagery and verbal practice[1]—enough to immediately contradict many easy generalizations, such as, that his poetry appeals mainly to the ear; enough to show why even the ideas in *Paradise Lost* outlast any intellectual analysis of their contradictions, since these ideas are conveyed in unmistakably concrete terms as well as argument. Original Sin, the fall from God's grace, is brought home to us by the *physical sense* of Satan's fall from Heaven, repeated and reported from beginning to end of *Paradise Lost*. Though the fall is the same presented from various points of view, Satan falls almost as often as the hero of *Finnegans Wake*. Beatitude itself Milton makes essentially pleasure in seeing, hearing, feeling, smelling, tasting God.[2] And this sense of supreme bliss

[1] No elaborate analysis of language is intended, but attention must be drawn to the impact of certain words, especially verbs, in Milton.

[2] See, among others, this passage:

> Thus while *God spake, ambrosial fragrance filled*
> All heaven, and in the blessed spirits elect
> *Sense of new joy ineffable diffused:*
> Beyond compare *the Son of God was seen*
> *Most glorious,* in him all his father shone
> *Substantially expressed,* and in his face
> Divine compassion *visibly appeared,*
> Love without end, and without measure grace
>
> . . . .

remains with us after we have forgotten God's sometimes disturbing display of rhetorical logic. Samson's protest

> why was the sight
> To such a tender ball as the eye confined?
> So obvious and so easy to be quenched,
> *And not as feeling through all parts diffused,*
> *That she might look at will through every pore?*
>
> S.A., 93–97

is much more than conceit in a poet who brings us alive at every pore.

In Milton's poetry as in our own experience we seldom receive any pure, isolated sense-impression. Mr. Eliot is among those who overstress Milton's reliance on the ear, remembering perhaps that our greatest contemporary master of language, James Joyce, relied upon his ear increasingly as blindness descended. Though by no means lacking in visual effects, he depends more than Milton on sound. Yet Joyce writes of oratory:

> how mielodorous thy belchant,
>
> F.W., 512

leaving sound "sysentangled" with the smell and taste of honey. The quality of the Lady's song-notes as heard by Comus is made remarkable in terms of other senses:

> How sweetly did they *float upon the wings*
> *Of silence, through the empty-vaulted night*
> *At every fall smoothing the raven down*
> *Of darkness till it smiled* . . .
>
> Comus, 248–51

This my long sufferance and my day of grace
They who neglect and scorn, shall never *taste*.

P.L., III, 135 ff.

Here the exquisite fusion of touch and motion and *plenitude* after emptiness is so intense that it trembles into sensuality, and this ecstasy, as frequently in Milton, culminates in involuntary *smile,* denoting complete gratification of the senses. Comus of course embodies sensuality; yet hear how the same song strikes the Spirit Attendant on the Lady's chastity:

> At last a soft and solemn *breathing* sound
> *Rose like a steam of rich distilled perfumes,*
> And *stole* upon the air, that *even silence*
> *Was took ere she was ware* . . .
>
> *Comus,* 554–57

Sound, with its accompanying sensation of actual breathing, is conveyed in terms of smell so seductive that along with the Attendant Spirit even silence is taken, ravished. Smell is related but not quite so close to sensuality as touch; whether or not Milton intends it, there is subtle differentiation between the song's effect on Comus and on the Attendant Spirit. We shall find that he invariably entangles these two senses along with sight in portraying sensuality, just as Shakespeare has Othello cry out:

> O thou weed,
> Who art so lovely fair and smell'st so sweet
> That the sense aches at thee . . .
>
> *Othello,* IV, ii, 67–69

Comus is the first poem in which Milton strikes out boldly for himself,[3] in which we can see him clearly

---

[3] *L'Allegro* and *Il Penseroso,* not only near perfect of their kind but a kind apart, are not so notably sensuous. An earlier version of this song-image appears, however, in *Il Penseroso* (56–58), where the nightingale's song smooths "the rugged brow of night."

assimilating influences[4] yet developing his own style and imagery. For the first time his extraordinary sensuous range—never cloying as Keats sometimes is—comes into full play, probably because the design of the poem provides a shield behind which he drops his youthful inhibitions without anxiety. *Comus* is on the surface so obstreperously moral that endowing physical seduction with poetic richness logically, if not actually, intensifies virtue's triumph.

Anticipating Satan's seduction, Comus tempts the thirsty Lady primarily through sight, smell, and taste:

> And first behold this cordial julep here
> *That flames, and dances in his crystal bounds*
> *With spirits of balm, and fragrant syrups mixed* . . .
> *Comus*, 672 ff.

More insidiously persuasive than his argument are his lavish images, "all to please and sate the curious taste." But surprisingly it is the pure Attendant Spirit who voices the most arresting sensuousness in his account of Sabrina's revival:

> And gave her to his daughters to *imbathe*
> *In nectared lavers strewed with asphodel,*
> *And through the porch and inlet of each sense*
> *Dropped in ambrosial oils till she revived* . . .
> *Comus*, 836–39

This healing spell is counterpart of evil magic, working so much in the same way as Comus' proffered transformation that there is pleasure on the surface of the whole

---

[4] See Tillyard and others. Shakespeare, Spenser, and Marlowe seem to me most clearly recognizable.

body (*imbathe*), in the smell and taste, in the very feel of the soothing oils penetrating each inlet.

That good and evil have this common meeting ground in the senses Milton is well aware, sometimes arbitrarily drawing a rational line (temperance) between legitimate and illegitimate delight, but never denying these avenues of truth without which his most spiritual verse would be sterile and cold. The Attendant Spirit shows how involuntary is the response to stimuli; for him and the virtuous, Milton like Shakespeare and Spenser assumes, without always accounting for it, rare purity of sense. He assumes the Platonic-Christian progression upward from matter to spirit, yet he never really divorces the two. There is danger of reversing direction, when

> The soul grows clotted by contagion,
> Imbodies, and imbrutes, till she quite lose
> The divine property of her first being
>
> . . . .
>
> As loath to leave the body that it loved,
> And linked itself by carnal sensuality
> To a degenerate and degraded state . . .
>
> *Comus,* 466 ff.

But eventually Milton un-Platonically "imbodies" if not "imbrutes" Heaven itself, for he grants the highest and most exquisite sensuous susceptibility and capacity to the upper reaches of his hierarchy, where his archangels

> All heart they live, all head, all eye, all ear,
> All intellect, all sense—
>
> *P.L.,* VI, 350–51

mingle in love with a superhuman variety and intensity possible only to those who can "assume what shape they please." Though all are rarefied, no physical quality is sloughed off in Heaven.

Knowledge of God comes to Milton through man's spark of divine reason aided by Revelation; but it enters the substance of his poetry most successfully as that blissful, far from ineffable state of knowing God through the porch and inlet of each sense, as tangible and perceptible as ambrosial oils. Else we should willingly deliver him over to the theologians.

2.

The Lady's song is only one among innumerable instances of his sensitivity to all forms of music. Music was in the air of the seventeenth century. For subtle accuracy of vocal sound Milton is inferior to Joyce, who made of sound a career; but he is the most accomplished musician of all English poets. Various choral harmonies of singing birds, running water, winds, instruments inevitably remind us of Spenser, whose trade-mark they are.

But Spenser cannot match the effect of the Lady's song on the two listeners, and his most elaborate harmonies are less precisely, more conventionally, imagined than Milton's organ music or symphonies:

> whence the sound
> Of instruments that made melodious chime
> Was heard, of harp and organ; and *who movĕd*
> *Their stops and chords was seen: his volant touch*
> *Instinct through all proportions low and high*
> *Fled and pursued transverse the resonant fugue.*
>
> P.L., XI, 558–63

As Milton interprets song in terms of smell and gives an actual sensation of the breathing necessary to phrase; so here we *see* the articulating fingers both *fleeing* and *pursuing* the fugue (which has assumed entity) and we *feel* at least a suggestion of touch on keys and strings. For the hand too becomes vocal:

> Circling the throne and singing, *while the hand*
> *Sung with the voice* . . .
>
> P.R., I, 171–72

Body and instrument fuse in a harmony of sound. Participation in the actual physical performance of the organist at his keyboard is quite distinct from the virtuoso mimicry of Tennyson. Milton not only does not attempt here to reproduce organ music; he leaves the notes to imagination, suggesting only the structure of a fugue. This startlingly immediate detail of the organist may be considered, strictly speaking, out of focus (though Milton's imagery is never merely photographic) in Adam's vision of the children of Cain at their varied pursuits. But it illustrates how Milton uses sound and vision not so much to imitate as to *shape* and to dramatize—in the sense that the image seems to be *happening* to us as we read it.[5]

More significant than reproduction in verse of actual song, instrumental music in obligato, musical perform-

[5] The most discriminating and detailed comment on the immediacy of Milton's sound and imagery I find in Arnold Stein's *Answerable Style*, 142 ff. Closest to the limited aspect of Milton's imagery which presently concerns me is Stein's excellent example of the shellfish: "To imagine a shellfish is not to imagine seeing it, but to imagine being it." Perhaps I can make my point clearer by adapting: "To imagine an organist is not to imagine hearing and seeing him *only*, but to imagine being him."

ance, is Milton's plastic and symbolical use of sound. Invariably, discord is associated with hostile forces; harmony, with God and goodness and the divine order. Though such symbolism is traditional, Milton's use of it is remarkably original. *Paradise Lost* is built with sound. Creation, wherever it occurs, is accompanied with rapturous harmony:

> Up he rode
> Followed with acclamation and the sound
> Symphonious of ten thousand harps that tuned
> Angelic harmonies: the earth, the air
> Resounded . . .
>
> P.L., VII, 557–61

Each of the Six Days is musically rounded out. Even in Hell when the Fallen Angels, true to their original nature, are engaged in constructive enterprise, harmonious music is present. Pandemonium rises to sound

> Of dulcet symphonies and voices sweet.
>
> P.L., I, 712

Conversely, clashing discord, like a harsh, physically painful Wagnerian motive, accompanies rebellion against God even in Heaven:

> And clamor such as heard in heaven till now
> Was never, arms on armor clashing *brayed*
> *Horrible discord* . . . all heaven
> Resounded, and had earth been then, all earth
> Had to her center shook.
>
> P.L., VI, 208 ff.

The *noise* of the new satanic artillery, as actively destructive as the explosion, eviscerates the air:

From those deep throated engines belched, whose
  roar
Emboweled with outrageous noise the air,
And all her entrails tore, disgorging foul
Their devilish glut . . .

P.L., VI, 586–89

And during the ensuing fall the vibration of sound
waves sets aquiver regions far beyond the universe:

Hell heard the unsufferable noise, hell saw
Heaven ruining from heaven and would have fled
Affrighted; but strict fate had cast too deep
Her dark foundations, and too fast had bound.

P.L., VI, 867–70

Not only is violence in Milton accompanied with
audible uproar, but all space becomes a sounding board
to convey vastness measured again and again by echoes
rebounding from almost infinite distances. The confines
of Hell cannot hold the multitudinous voices of the
Fallen Angels, which *tear* the concave and, bellowing
through the deep, frighten even Chaos and old Night
who are attuned to discord as their natural element.
Especially is Chaos, where visual sharpness is impossible in the murk, created through repeated reverberation on the ear. The sounds are as palpable and shock-
ing as a blow:

At length a universal hubbub wild
Of *stunning* sounds and voices all confused
Borne through the hollow dark *assaults* his ear
With loudest vehemence . . .

P.L., II, 951–54

We shall find later that this portrayal of sound not just as impression perceived but as waves in motion *striking* the ear fits into other kinetic imagery to create the remarkable movement and energy of Milton's verse.

When critics emphasize the aural in Milton they are usually thinking primarily of the sound of the lines themselves, the "apt numbers, fit quantity of syllables, and [sustained music of] the sense variously drawn out from one verse into another"; and of the way sound values dictate so often Milton's choice of words. At this point it is impossible any longer to separate, except temporarily and theoretically, aural from oral.

For words must be formed in the mouth and throat and propelled by breath before they can impinge on the ear; and though it may seem outlandish on first consideration, probably Milton derived as much pleasure from the actual formation of words on the tongue, the sense of muscular expansion of the diaphragm to expel air through vocal cords, as from the sound they make. His poetry—as the Lady's song already shows—is full of the physical sensation of inhaling and exhaling, which he celebrates over and over as much too important to be taken for granted. The land "breathes forth elixir pure"; Satan inhales this, "breathing smell of field and grove"; Satan speaks, exhaling a sigh, and the sense of outbreathing is as strong as the emotion; even the moon *exhales* nourishment; the east at dawn *exhales* light; the sun *inhales* and *exhales*; Pandemonium rises with the ease of expelled breath; God breathes forth immortal love and breathes in the odors of sacrifice. And so on endlessly.

All writers are orally sensitive. Where most of us

regard words as simply means and nothing else, a poet loves words largely for themselves, their separate identity, their physical formation, their feel, taste, sound. Reading any poet aloud is the full revelation he requires. Reading Milton aloud is a challenge physically exhausting. Yeats is the only other poet who requires such lung capacity, such breath control for difficult and sustained phrasing, such resonance. Both are fond of the orotund and savor words as much by larynx as by ear. Yeats' Byzantium poems recapture the plangent opening of the Second Book of *Paradise Lost:*

> High on a throne of royal state, which far
> Outshone the wealth of Ormus and of Ind,
> Or where the gorgeous east with richest hand
> Showers on her kings barbaric pearl and gold . . .

This dependence of words on the whole breathing apparatus is more significant than pleasure in the physical adjustments necessary to form the simplest word, which is not only a basic distinction of man from brute by this capacity for intelligible sounds, but a triumphant demonstration of life itself. As long as we form words, we are consciously alive; elaborate choice makes us creatively alive. *Spirit* is from *spiritus* (breath). Thus words are intimately connected with the source of our being. They are also the material of wisdom, for thoughts must be articulated to be grasped or communicated:

> Wisest of men; *from whose mouths issued forth*
> *Mellifluous streams* that watered all the schools
> Of academics old and new . . .
>
> P.R., IV, 276–78

They are, even when scorned, concrete guarantors of immortality:

> And what delight to be by such extolled,
> *To live upon their tongues and be their talk,*
> Of whom to be dispraised were no small praise?
> P.R., III, 54–56

Dr. Johnson's advice to Hannah More is more emphatic: "Never mind whether they praise or abuse your writings; anything is tolerable, *except oblivion.*"

But of course it is not man's word only that concerns us, but God's:

> And reason; since his *word* all things produced.
> P.R., III, 122

This is the source of all power:

> My *word,* my wisdom, and effectual might.
> P.L., III, 170

God's voice dominates *Paradise Lost* and *Paradise Regained,* loved and feared, since it bears life or death; since without it nothing that is is. The Creation we shall find simply uttering the "Omnific Word," [6] "for Chaos heard his voice." And the Bible, Infinite Truth made miraculously finite in the language of men, is identified with God made flesh in Christ:

> And thou my *word,* begotten Son, by thee
> This I perform, *speak thou,* and be it done.
> P.L., VII, 163–64

---

[6] Milton's choice of *omnific* is not fully explained by Latinism or sound value. He probably liked the exhilarating, explosive sensation of actually *saying* the word. Arnold Stein (*Answerable Style,* 143) mentions "elaborate mouthing" for *comic* effect, but many of Milton's most serious passages require equally elaborate mouthing.

No wonder Milton of all poets glories most in the word and gives free rein to his delight in the oral potentialities of man in their whole range from complex physical adjustments to that inspiration or inbreathing and subsequent exhaling the wisdom of God. Words are to him concrete manifestations of *spiritus* in all its variety of meaning.

We cannot overstress a fundamental truth about Milton which we find endlessly proliferated in his work. At his most creative, he accepts the whole range from the physical, specifically the senses, to the ultimate Divine as *absolutely unbroken*. This glad acceptance means that he is free to speak of any order of being (extending to inanimate matter) in identical sensuous terms as the great common denominator. For our purposes there is no need to query this or to attempt logical reconciliation with his intellectual beliefs,[7] since we are concerned entirely with his practice and with his remarkable, though not completely successful attempt to make all that he has to say at once perceptible through the senses and intelligible to the mind. Few poets (Lucretius, Dante,

---

[7] Milton's own attempts to explain himself seem often afterthoughts, rationalizing. One source and example is the Bible, particularly the Old Testament; for this sensuousness and anthropomorphism are elements in Hebraic poetry. The Jewish mind was, according to W. K. Lowther Clark (*Concise Bible Commentary*, 230), "non-dualistic and did not think in terms of the contrast between material and spiritual. The Jews thought rather of man functioning as a whole."

Ultimately, the answer lies in Milton's own temperament, which made the characteristic Hebraic blend of ascetic spirituality and sensuality peculiarly congenial, and explains the equal attraction he found in ascetic Plato and sensual Ovid.

Sensuousness is almost invariably too weak a word for Milton's deep involvement with the senses; yet I am aware that sensuality has generally a stronger connotation of moral condemnation than I usually give it.

Spenser, occasionally Wordsworth) have come so close to making what are ordinarily abstract concepts thus tangible.

There are times when by this method he anticipates Joyce's consciously exploited capacity of writing simultaneously, as if in a new dimension of language, on several levels. Joyce's most unblinking and brutally physiological explorations are so entwined with intellectual and spiritual processes (such as his interlocking cannibalism, the communion service, and adolescent sexual experiments) that none of these elements has separate identity, nor can such a passage be condemned as obscene without qualification. Milton does not of course go so far, in some respects not so far as the more schematic Spenser; yet many of his bold identifications are of the same order and cannot be judged simply.

So it is that when we consider other than verbal manifestations of oral we find not only enmeshing with other senses than taste, especially touch and smell, but figurative levels of meaning almost as automatic as sense reactions. This tendency in Milton is so marked that he speaks of Satan, maneuvering for his temptation, as *tasting* Christ, not merely testing. The basic physiological function of oral is of course nourishment. Like breath, food is essential to life. I have already inescapably touched on nourishment in illustrating the verbal, for oral faculties are inseparable and Milton delights in multiplying these complex familiar relationships. Words are a kind of food. Belial's "tongue dropped manna."

Most poets take this for granted, but Milton from beginning to end is preoccupied with eating—literal and figurative. We remember indulgently "no fear lest dinner cool"; yet we must read *Paradise Lost* and its great companion poems several times to realize how constant is the taking of food. Neither the denizens of Paradise nor of Heaven miss a meal, invariably described with unabashed enjoyment. As for the angels:

> food alike those pure
> Intelligential substances require
> As doth your rational; and *both contain*
> *Within them every lower faculty*
> *Of sense, whereby they hear, see, smell,*
>   *touch, taste,*
> *Tasting concoct, digest, assimilate,*
> And corporeal to incorporeal turn.
>
>   P.L., V, 407–13

A. J. A. Waldock (*Paradise Lost and its Critics*, 108) finds this sort of thing the more reprehensible because Milton believed in his absurdities. I find occasional absurdity a small price to pay, since his passionate belief in the identity of spiritual and physical fertilizes such a rare harvest.

Whatever is created needs food. The nourishing sun must in turn be replenished:

> The sun that light imparts to all, *receives*
> *From all his alimental recompense*
> *In humid exhalations,* and at even
> Sups with the ocean . . .
>
>   P.L., V, 423–26

That this is no passing poetic fancy but a central belief becomes clear when we find three books later in Adam's account of his first consciousness:

> I found me laid
> In balmy sweat, which with his beams the sun
> Soon dried, and *on the reeking moisture fed.*
>
>   P.L., VIII, 254–56

In the general scheme of a key passage on nourishment in the Fifth Book "the grosser feeds the purer."

All creatures not only eat but are themselves devoured. Eating can cause as much fear as pleasure, the mouth become destructive. In *Samson Agonistes* at one point the Chorus voices this primitive fear of being eaten:

> Best keep together here, lest running thither
> We unawares run into *danger's mouth.*
>
>   S.A., 1521–22

And *Paradise Lost* is filled with the terror of being swallowed up by misery, disaster, chaos, oblivion. Sin and Death are eternally drooling with hunger, ravenous, insatiable. The grave is forever waiting to be glutted. Anticipating Tennyson's Darwin-foreshadowing nightmare of nature red in tooth and claw, Milton frequently draws on primordial horror of cannibalism and expresses it through actual nausea. The Universe revolts physiologically and psychologically when Adam and Eve eat the forbidden fruit. Just as the Fallen Angels reject "with spattering noise" the bitter ashes in Hell, on the final triumph of Satan over Eve, Milton reminds us of Thyestes unwittingly eating his children at Atreus' infamous meal:

> The sun, *as from Thyestean banquet,* turned
> His course intended . . .
>
>   P.L., X, 688–89

In *Paradise Lost* gulfs and yawning chasms and mouths threaten on every hand. Occasionally terror of cannibalism, of being swallowed up by the terrible unknown, becomes sexual fear, the male's fear of the praying mantis female:

> the void profound
> Of unessential night receives him next
> Wide gaping, and with utter loss of being
> *Threatens him, plunged in that abortive gulf*
>
> . . . .
>
> To perish rather, *swallowed up and lost*
> *In the wide womb of uncreated night . . .*
>
> P.L., II, 438–41; 149–50

But this heritage from our obscure primitive past has also a positive spiritual value, the Communion, eating the body and drinking the blood of Christ.[8] For by the instinctive process of man's thinking and imagining, the soul too requires nourishment and the mind *feeds* on thoughts

> that voluntary move
> Harmonious numbers . . .
>
> P.L., III, 37–38

While the "thirst I had of knowledge" has become so familiar that we have lost any sense of figure, Raphael elaborates in alimentary terms:

> But *knowledge is as food,* and needs no less
> Her temperance over appetite, to know
> In measure what the mind may well contain,

[8] The oral theme is of course dominant in Joyce, whose Finn is also Osiris and Christ. Eaten by his children, Finn is resurrected in them.

> Oppresses else with surfeit, and soon turns
> Wisdom to folly, as nourishment to wind.
>
> *P.L.*, VII, 126–30

And Adam:

> Yet not so strictly hath our Lord imposed
> Labor, as to debar us when we need
> Refreshment, whether food, or talk between,
> *Food of the mind,* or this sweet intercourse
> Of looks and smiles . . .
>
> *P.L.*, IX, 235–39

But Adam, as well as Eve, "knew not eating death." Adam forgets the sense of Raphael's words when, after they have eaten the fruit, with unconscious irony he compliments Eve on the new food:

> Eve, now I see thou art exact of taste,
> And elegant, *of sapience no small part,*
> *Since to each meaning savor we apply,*
> *And palate call judicious* . . .
>
> *P.L.*, IX, 1017–20

Milton and his age recognized at once what we in this latter day have forgotten, that the root of *sapience* is "to taste." And so Samson's casual taunt to Harapha of Gath, who has come to see the paragon of might—"The way *to know* were not to see but *taste*"—strikes at the root of human experience and might be transposed to Satan's mouth as he reasons with Eve.

There are concealed surprises in Milton's most magnificent banquet, which Satan prepares to tempt the forty-days-famished Christ in the Second Book of *Paradise Regained*, an elaboration of Lucullan feast, Veronese's baroque "Last Supper," and Ariel's mock-banquet

in the *Tempest*. The assault is not only on hunger and
delicate palate, but also on eye and nose and ear, for
there is music, perfume, and even a fillip to sex:

> Our Saviour lifting up his eyes beheld
> In ample space under the broadest shade
> A table richly spread, in regal mode,
> With dishes piled, and meats of noblest sort
> And savor, beasts of chase, or fowl of game,
> In pastry built, or from the spit, or boiled,
> Grisamber-steamed; all fish from sea or shore,
> Freshet, or purling brook, of shell or fin,
> And exquisitest name, for which was drained
> Pontus and Lucrine bay, and Afric coast.
> *Alas how simple, to these cates compared,*
> *Was that crude apple that diverted Eve!*
> And at a stately sideboard by the wine
> That fragrant smell diffused, in order stood
> Tall stripling youths rich clad, of fairer hue
> Than Ganymed or Hylas, distant more
> Under the trees now tripped, now solemn stood
> Nymphs of Diana's train, and naiades
> With fruits and flowers from Amalthea's horn,
> And ladies of the Hesperides, that seemed
> Fairer than feigned of old, or fabled since
> Of fairy damsels met in forest wide
> By knights of Logres, or of Lyonnesse,
> Lancelot or Pelleas, or Pellenore,
> And all the while harmonious airs were heard
> Of chiming strings, or charming pipes and winds
> Of gentlest gale Arabian odors fanned
> From their soft wings, and Flora's earliest smells.
> P.R., II, 338–65

Epicurean Milton, for all his warnings about unfer-
mented liquors and simple fare, can rival Keats with
delicacies,

so contrived as not to mix
Tastes, not well joined, inelegant, but bring
Taste after taste upheld with kindliest change . . .

P.L., V, 334–36

When he wants he offers *dulcet creams, rubied nectar*. Yet unlike the feast on St. Agnes Eve or his own practice elsewhere, Milton here dwells more on the rarity and difficulty of procuring and preparing these strange delicacies; and curiously the oral pleasure is derived in this instance less from the foods contemplated than from the taste of the actual words: *Grisamber-steamed, exquisitest name, Ganymed, Hylas, Amalthea, Hesperides, Logres, Lyonnesse, Lancelot, Pelleas, Pellenore.*

3.

With Milton the temporary dominance of one sense over others is only that of a melody over its accompaniment; more often his effects are blending chords. Taste itself is mainly a combination of texture and smell, intensified in Satan's banquet by adding to the natural savor of food the Grisamber perfume cooked with it. Smell of meats and wines mingles with "Arabian odors" so dear to Milton, both of imported spices and of early spring—a keener sensuous memory of Horton days than appears in *L'Allegro*. This passage from *Paradise Regained* is the only one in all four books in which smell occurs. Smell is nearly as rare in *Samson Agonistes*. But the rest of Milton's poetry reveals for a man an abnormal sensitivity to the whole range of odors from carrion to delicatest perfume.

More keenly susceptible, more aware also of decorum,

Milton is oddly not so discriminating about smells as Spenser. Invariably he chooses the freshness of early morning or after rain for his flower smells, and he shows disgust with seventeenth century urban sanitation:

> Where houses thick and sewers annoy the air.
> *P.L.,* IX, 446

But Milton, who mentions with un-Spenserian circumlocution the smell of sweaty labor or Adam's "reeking moisture," seems to enjoy the sense of smell for itself, and so does not suggest the physical and spiritual revulsion that Spenser would give to the stenches of Hell, Asmodeus' "fishy fume," or especially to Death whiffing his prey:

> such a scent I draw
> Of carnage, prey innumerable, and taste
> The savor of death . . . . .
> . . . with delight he snuffed the smell
> Of mortal change on earth . . . lured
> With scent of living carcasses designed
> For death . . . .
> So scented the grim feature, and upturned
> His nostril wide into the murky air . . .
> *P.L.,* X, 267 ff.

Milton enters wholeheartedly into Death's anticipatory pleasure.

He never tires of "fertile earth after soft showers," the sweet "breath of morn," "fragrant leaf," "sweet-smelling herbs." And surely only Milton with his gargantuan appetite would speak of rich compacted odors as *enormous bliss.* Again we find that telltale *smile* of uninhibited sensuous gratification in this best of many Arabian passages:

> now gentle gales
> Fanning their odoriferous wings dispense
> Native perfumes, and whisper whence they stole
> Those balmy spoils . . . .
> Sabean odors from the spicy shore
> Of Araby the blest, with such delay
> Well pleased they slack their course, and many a
>   league
> *Cheered with the grateful smell old ocean smiles.*
>   P.L., IV, 156 ff.

Playing on the volatility of smell in a passage which is partly rationalization, partly semi-serious reworking of a traditional simile, Raphael uses the universality and refinement of fragrance to explain to Adam how matter rises into soul:

> Each in their several active spheres assigned,
> Till body up to spirit work, in bounds
> Proportioned to each kind. So from the root
> Springs lighter the green stalk, from thence the
>   leaves
> More airy, last the bright consummate flower
> *Spirits odorous breathes* . . .
>   P.L., V, 477 ff.

But Milton is more convincing about smell when less self-conscious. The two appearances of his great heroines, Eve and Dalila (smell is inevitably part of woman's seductiveness), in the very quality of their fragrance draw a fine distinction between the natural beauty of innocence and the contrived beauty of artifice:

Beyond his hope, Eve separate he spies,
Veiled in a cloud of fragrance, where she stood.

P.L., IX, 424–25

Eve, clothed only in her own sweetness blended with the smell of Eden's flowers, is thus met by Satan. Whereas Dalila enters

Courted by all the winds that hold them play,
An *amber scent* of odorous perfume
Her harbinger . . .

S.A., 719–21

In each case the smell is so intense as to be visible—as a transparent veil for Eve, as a delicate, sophisticated off-tint for Dalila (ambergris-amber).

Naturally, angels being of a higher order exude rarer smell. When God sends Raphael down to tutor Adam:

Like Maia's son he stood,
And shook his plumes, that heavenly fragrance filled
The circuit wide . . . .
Into the blissful field, through groves of myrrh,
And flowering odors, cassia, nard, and balm;
A wilderness of sweets . . .

P.L., V, 285 ff.

The highest reach and rarest distillation is God himself, in whose image both angels and men are made. One of the greatest pleasures of being in the divine presence is His delicate perfume. His "altar breathes ambrosial odors and ambrosial flowers"; when He speaks fragrance fills all Heaven.

Besides being the source of divine sweetness, God appreciates smells most—the breath of plants, animals, Adam, Eve:

> In Eden on the humid flowers, that breathed
> Their morning incense, *when all things that breathe,*
> From earth's great altar send up silent praise
> To the creator, and *his nostrils fill*
> *With grateful smell* . . .
>
> P.L., IX, 193–97

When Noah sacrificed the beasts and fowls "the Lord smelled a sweet savour." Unquestionably, the prototype of Milton's capacity for smelling and his uninhibited catholicity is God of the Old Testament. In versifying Abel's sacrifice Milton enjoys specifying how the very "inwards and their fat" send up to God a "grateful steam." His own robust taste for smell, far surpassing Browning's Bishop of St. Praxed, rivals that of ancient Hebrew poets.

More telling than all these clustered images, however, is the instinctive naturalness with which the poet who has Satan *taste* Christ also mentions the *smell* of peace (*P.L.*, XI, 38).

Irresistible appeal to the nose, especially when joined with appeal to the eye, leads instinctively to touch. Milton makes beautiful use of these chain reactions in his portrayal of temptation in Eden:

> A bough of *fairest fruit that downy smiled,*
> New gathered, and *ambrosial smell diffused.*
> P.L., IX, 851–52

Man reaches out to pluck not only because his mouth waters and he wants to possess, but also because he cannot resist the desire to feel that soft "downy" bloom before sinking teeth into the mellow flesh of the fruit.

When touch involves reaching out, is active rather

than passive, it partakes inevitably of the kinetic, at least to the variable extent that we sense muscles rippling under the skin or the resistance of outside objects to movement. I make this suggestion in passing for those who happen instinctively to feel the gathering of muscles preparatory to physical action such as Satan's:

> Due entrance he disdained, and in contempt,
> At one slight bound high overleaped all bound,
> Of hill or highest wall, and sheer within
> Lights on his feet . . . . . .
> Leaps o'er the fence with ease into the fold.
>
> *P.L.*, IV, 180 ff.

While Satan makes his way over strange terrain, as he "swims or sinks, or wades, or creeps, or flies," we shall see how remarkably Milton uses this sense of effort and movement to energize the poem.

When Satan falls after the third and last temptation, leaving Christ perilously poised on the pinnacle of the Temple—

> straight a fiery globe
> Of angels on full sail of wing flew nigh,
> Who on their plumy vanes *received him soft*
> From his uneasy station, and upbore
> *As on a floating couch* through the blithe air.
>
> *P.R.*, IV, 581–85

Here a sense of pressure is added. This same pressure under enormous weight is one means of building Satan's superheroic size:

> Aloft, incumbent on the dusky air
> *That felt unusual weight* . . .
>
> *P.L.*, I, 226–27

More persistently than most poets, Milton animates the inanimate. Again in the Sixth Book "the passive air" bears up under the weight of the marching host. If he does not visualize his huge angels in specific detail, he is always conscious of their size and cubic displacement and pressure. This passive touch felt by the air is akin to Sabrina's sensation on being imbathed with oils. Milton can be extremely subtle, portraying the delicate, barely palpable weight of drowsy eyelids soft as dewfall:

> the timely *dew of sleep*
> Now falling *with soft slumberous weight* inclines
> Our eyelids . . .
>
> *P.L.*, IV, 614–16

Through this involuntary touch on the surface of the body we perceive temperature changes, to which Milton is so sensitive that he notes them both casually and for specific purposes. The contrast between sensual Comus and chaste Sabrina we feel directly in the sudden shift from hot to cold when Sabrina begins her spell to free the Lady from enslavement:

> Next this marble venomed seat
> *Smeared with gums of glutinous heat*
> I touch with chaste *palms moist and cold* . . .
>
> *Comus*, 915–17

And notice, it is *sticky* hot and *damp* cold. To catalogue ubiquitous "kindly heat," "vital warmth," "cold sudden damp"—most indicating shifts of emotional key—would be tedious. But the slight drop in temperature when a cloud suddenly cuts off the sun:

> A shelter and *a kind of shading cool*
> *Interposition, as a summer's cloud,*
>
> P.R., III, 221–22

brings home poignantly Satan's maximum respite from God's white-hot ire; the only transitory relief that even Christ, by interposing in his favor, could grant him.

In God's wrath and the constant holocaust of Hell heat is fiercely destructive; it can be creative, too, as we see from a passing reminiscence in *Samson Agonistes* (549) of Moses' fiery rod producing life-giving water from stone. Heat and touch are also closely associated in Milton's mind with creativity. On one occasion this creative heat (surely "more warmth than Adam needs" is intentional humor), drives Adam inside his Eden bower at noon:

> in the door he sat
> Of his cool bower, while now *the mounted sun*
> *Shot down direct his fervid rays to warm*
> *Earth's inmost womb,* more warmth than Adam needs . . .
>
> P.L., V, 299–302

This fertilizing power of the male principle Milton again and again attributes to the sun, God's deputy, that foments and warms, the female being earth and ocean— a traditional concept, to be sure, but never made more ardently graphic.

Touch frequently, almost inevitably with Milton, sweeps sensuousness into sensuality. When in her effort to placate Samson, Dalila asks:

> Let me approach at least, and *touch thy hand,*

he explodes:

Not for thy life, lest *fierce remembrance wake*
My sudden rage to tear thee joint by joint.

S.A., 951 ff.

He cannot bear that betraying touch again, knowing too
well how thoroughly she has earlier subdued him by
touch—even to the symbolical castration of shorn hair
and blind eyes. Through the sense of touch, we recall,
sensual Comus perceives the Lady's song, *smoothing the
raven down of darkness till it smiled,* whereas the Attendant Spirit responds with the more rarefied sense of smell.
Belial in *Paradise Regained* (II, 163 ff.) knows even
better than Samson the spell of woman's touch, which

> hath the power to soften and tame
> Severest temper, *smooth the ruggedest brow,*
> *Enerve, and with voluptuous hope dissolve* . . .

As we shall see more fully in his portrayal of creation
and temptation, Milton makes no bones about the cen-
trality of touch. Even in a state of innocence Adam
learns quickly:

> Thus have I told thee all my state, and brought
> My story to the sum of earthly bliss
> Which I enjoy, and must confess to find
> *In all things else delight indeed, but such*
> *As used or not, works in the mind no change,*
> Nor vehement desire, these delicacies
> I mean of taste, sight, smell, herbs, fruits, and
>   flowers,
> Walks, and the melody of birds; *but here*
> *Far otherwise, transported I behold,*
> *Transported touch; here passion first I felt,*
> Commotion strange, in all enjoyments else

Superior and unmoved, *here only weak*
Against the charm of beauty's powerful glance.
P.L., VIII, 521–33

Adam's sense of touch is so keen that he not only feels
but *sees* it (I *behold*); and "beauty's powerful glance"
is palpable. To the futile question, "Which sense is
most dominant in Milton?," one may well answer,
"whichever sense occupies him at any one moment, and
almost never any single sense."

4.

Above all others, most would say, Milton himself
ranks the sense of sight which he lost and which he
laments in familiar passages in prose and verse, most
movingly in the sonnets, *Paradise Lost,* and *Samson
Agonistes,* with most finality in this characteristic
(though not original) transposition from sight to sound
wherein blindness is intensified by deafness in a vast
quiet of planetary eclipse:

The sun to me is *dark*
And *silent* as the moon.

S.A., 86–87

Yet on the evidence of his poetry of whom can it be more
fittingly said than of Milton that

though sight be lost,
Life yet hath many solaces, enjoyed
Where other senses want not their delights,
S.A., 914–16

especially since his memory was stored with the visual
imagery of some forty years' observation before he lost
his sight?

Since he keeps reminding us of blindness, understandably critics, overlooking the bold and precise visualization of a neo-Ptolemaic Universe in *Paradise Lost*, sometimes attribute blurred visual details to cataract or deficient imagination rather than deliberate attempt to portray vastness and grandeur invisible even through man's ingenious optic glasses. Instead of defending his visual imagery[9] and combating the argument that physical infirmity drove Milton back on hearing, let us forget for the moment that he is blind and consider the extraordinary role of the eye in his poetry.

It is ablaze with eyes from beginning to end, like that mystic chariot of Christ drawn by angels:

> from the fourfold visaged four,
> *Distinct with eyes,* and from the living wheels
> Distinct alike *with multitude of eyes,*
> One spirit in them ruled, and *every eye*
> *Glared lightning,* and shot forth pernicious fire
> Among the accursed, that withered all their strength,
> And of their wonted vigor left them drained,
> Exhausted, spiritless, afflicted, fallen.
>
> *P.L.*, VI, 845–52

To Milton the eye is much more than a delicate lens for registering suitable stimuli; it is a character in the drama, acting and acted upon. Beyond all other senses Adam ranks touch. Samson says that the way to know is "not to see but taste." Yet Milton, not just because

---

[9] An admirably cogent defense has already been made by D. C. Allen, *The Harmonious Vision*, 95–109. The core of his essay is an account of Renaissance theories of light and light symbolism with which Milton was conversant.

blindness in maturity makes him a special case but because of the magic power associated with eyes since primordial times, grants to the eye all faculties including touch and taste.

As the most obviously expressive human feature he uses it constantly to characterize. Adam has an *eye sublime*, declaring absolute rule. At the very *sight* of Christ, wild beasts grow mild. In God's face divine compassion, mercy, and justice *visibly* appear. Satan's eyes betray shifting emotions: *baleful, sparkling blazed; cruel but cast signs of remorse; aghast* and *aghast and sad; commanding; tearful* as only angels' are. The eye reveals and reads the soul.

In Milton the eye has intense energy as well as delicate receptivity; it is both masculine and feminine. That the Fallen Angels *cast* wanton eyes on the daughters of men, if this were an isolated instance, might be mere convention; but not in a context where eyes persistently *are thrown, bent down*; where they *pursue, dart fire, rove without rein*; where God's eyes, usurping another sense, become a fire *devouring* the welcome sacrifice:

> His offering soon propitious fire from heaven
> *Consumed with nimble glance*, and grateful
>   steam . . .
>
> P.L., XI, 441–42

This strong association of looking and devouring is even more striking when eyes and glut in conjunction produce vicariously the significant smile of gratification:

> Thou *at the sight*
> Pleased, out of heaven shalt *look down and smile*,

> While by thee raised I ruin all my foes,
> Death last, and with his carcass *glut the grave*.
>
> > P.L., III, 256–59

We have seen how Milton when thinking of sapience automatically recalls its root, *to taste*. He regards the eye as a feeder of knowledge. The exploring, prying eye is from infancy a chief tool of man's curiosity to know. No less is this true of incorrigible Satan, who, antedating Adam, offers the first Miltonic case study of man's instincts. Revealing, just after his recovery in Hell from the Fall, the rumor of earth's creation, Satan confides to his followers:

> Thither, *if but to pry*, shall be perhaps
> Our first eruption . . .
>
> > P.L., I, 655–56

Later he dissembles to Uriel, God's *sharpest sighted*, but at least honestly expresses this basic drive of curiosity:

> *Unspeakable desire to see*, and know
> All these his wondrous works . . .
> That I may find him, and *with secret gaze*,
> Or *open admiration* him behold . . .
>
> > P.L., III, 662 ff.

At this point Satan has just had his first unobstructed view of the universe; it is ours, too, for significantly we see it first through his eyes and enter it first with him who is already tainted by Original Sin. Here Milton, blind though he is, precisely visualizes the panorama and shifting point of view as he focuses Satan's eager eyes, which first *look down*, then *round survey*, then *view in breadth*, until above all the sun, the "lordly eye" of heaven, *allured his eye.* Finally, the supernaturally clear air *sharpening his visual ray* (Dante with a difference), Satan focuses on Uriel in the infinite distance.

Taken in by Satan's hypocrisy (invisible to all but God), Uriel accepts Satan's word that this new knowledge is to be put to its proper use—glorifying God. But the same insatiable curiosity which leads to discovery, knowledge, science, civilization is also the root of Original Sin, as Milton with all his passion for these ends takes pains to point out. We have just seen Satan as a stout Balboa discovering God's new handiwork. Shortly after, as he is reduced to eavesdropping and spying on Adam and Eve, his discovering eye degenerates to peeping from the secret shrubbery. Envying Adam Eve, and Eve her innocence and both their sexual fulfillment, he becomes a voyeur:

> and pressed her matron lip
> With kisses pure: *aside the devil turned*
> *For envy, yet with jealous leer malign*
> *Eyed them askance . . .*
>
> P.L., IV, 501–504

"Set women *in his eye*" is sensual Belial's advice in *Paradise Regained* to tempt Christ, for Belial knows that the eye touches by anticipation a coveted object. Eve and Adam are first led to covet the forbidden fruit through the eye, and are led to touch and taste it in order to see more, to know more:

> Ye eat thereof, *your eyes that seem so clear,*
> *Yet are but dim* . . . .

This is the argument that sticks in Eve's mind when Satan's sophistries are done:

Fixed on the fruit she gazed, *which to behold*
Might tempt alone . . .

This is the argument which she relays to Adam:

This tree is not as we are told, a tree
Of danger tasted, nor to evil unknown
Opening the way, but *of divine effect*
To open eyes . . .

Adam, knowing well the great danger in "only coveting
to eye" much less eat, nonetheless eats too. And the
eye, the initial betrayer previously of Satan, also first
reveals the change in the universe:

but that false fruit
Far other operation first displayed,
Carnal desire inflaming, *he on Eve*
Began to cast lascivious eyes, she him
As wantonly repaid . . .

P.L., IX, 706 ff.

Thus by inevitable progression are we led to the multitudinous troop of his children which greets Adam's
eyes when at the end of the poem Michael leads him in
a dream to look upon the future—men whose eyes
"rove without rein" and lustful women who "troll the
tongue, and roll the eye."

To an extraordinary extent Puritan Milton[10] elaborates
this sensual role of the eye, and in so doing touches inevitably on the eye's ambiguous, primordial sexuality,

---

[10] Until the thirties and until scholars like the Hallers began demonstrating that Puritanism in the seventeenth century is not synonymous
with narrow bigotry, the tendency was to claim Milton as a pure
Renaissance figure.

which Joyce much more deliberately exploits in man's temptations and falls throughout *Finnegans Wake*. We have already seen that the sun in *Paradise Lost* is always male, the earth female. It is not surprising to find that the sun's dominance is exercised through his *lordly eye*, whose "magnetic beam" simultaneously dispenses essential light, keeps the constellations circling at proper distance in their orbits, and, usurping touch,

> gently warms
> The universe, and to each inward part
> With gentle penetration, though unseen,
> Shoots invisible virtue even to the deep.
>
> P.L., III, 583–86

We shall find later that this curious phallic symbolism of the eye can also be aggressive and destructive, like those frightening and paralyzing eyes of Christ's mystic chariot.

The eye can easily short-circuit in narcissism. Contemplating with satisfaction one's own virtue was good Renaissance practice and explains many passages in Milton which strike us now as insufferably self-complacent. Yet Milton, whom we suspect of creating Adam as much in his own as in God's image, curiously adapts the story of Narcissus to Eve. Almost immediately Adam pines for a mate, whereas Eve has to be prodded (like Joyce's heroine) from her first love, her own image in the lake:

> *there I had fixed*
> *Mine eyes till now*, and pined with vain desire,
> Had not a voice thus warned me . . .
>
> P.L., IV, 465–7

But Eve is not the first to show the self-regarding eye.
According to his daughter-mistress, it is narcissism which
causes Satan to fall in love with her:

> Thyself in me thy perfect image viewing.
>
> P.L., II, 764

Sin, after the manner of Athena, is born full-blown from
Satan's head the moment he has a rebellious thought
against God; the resulting duality makes possible his
looking upon her, then the love embrace producing
Death. This allegory is easy and satisfying: Satan and
Sin, and we may add Death, are one—a kind of unholy
trinity opposed to the Holy.

The mirror-eye is inevitable in Milton's scheme, where
God Himself loves Christ as the reflection of His own
glory and perfection. In a masculine theogony, the
Trinity is the first step in creation (granted that the
essence, the unmanifest can have for us no meaning),
enabling God to know Himself by creating Logos, the
Son, leaving the Holy Ghost an ambiguous role and
variably attributed sex. On the basis of some Old Testament and apocryphal passages, Spenser makes Sapience a
woman, but Milton usually[11] identifies Wisdom directly
with God, more frequently in terms of *voice* but also of
eye. As Athens, the fount of Greek wisdom, is for him
the "eye of Greece," so God the Omniscient has "un-
sleeping eyes," is the "eternal eye."

Writing in our time on this same theme of the Fall
and Original Sin, Joyce, who also seeks order in Chaos

[11] At the beginning of the Seventh Book of *Paradise Lost* Wisdom is
sister to Urania, the Heavenly Muse. Milton is probably thinking of
Proverbs 8.

and as firmly commits himself to the masculine Word, nonetheless delights in primeval Lilith and cabalistic theories, eschewing clarity for constant flux and coalescence of opposites. But as he pries into the secret of our past lives, Milton's genius for basic order and simplicity and clarity leads him to compromise with the straightforward account of creation in Genesis and, after wise deliberation, with the already outmoded Ptolemaic system. His own attitude toward this system and the extent of his astronomical knowledge have been amply investigated. As sophisticated in his own day as Joyce was in ours, Milton probably deliberately chose Ptolemy in much the same spirit that Joyce chose the four-part cycle of eighteenth century Giambattista Vico's outmoded *La Scienza Nuova*. In passing Milton shows awareness of Copernicus and of traditional treatments of creation, and for details draws on less orthodox Hebrew, cabalistic, patristic theories. Nostalgia for ancient matriarchy is as foreign to him as is the Restoration.

Warning of the danger in the powerful, restless eye with its destructive potentialities, he is too much the scientist to resist the eye's extension by microscope and telescope. His allusions to Galileo's experiments and "optic tube" are familiar; less known is Satan's "airy microscope" (*P.R.*, IV, 57). Is not man in thus exalting his own eye (*eye* equals *I*) unconsciously trying to equal the "eternal eye," and could it have crossed Milton's mind that in creating so grand a universe in *Paradise Lost* he like Satan is anxious to rival God?

Certainly a psychiatrist turned loose on *Paradise Lost* might be tempted to diagnose Milton's preoccupation with vastness—these obsessive visions of impossibly

gigantic angels, with shields bigger than a magnified
moon, staffs and spears so tall that they require imaginative arithmetic multiplying Norwegian pines and ship-
masts, these prodigious womb-like gulfs and chasms,
this Brobdingnagian hurtling of mountains and cliffs—
as macropsia, a visual distortion indicating deep psychic
disturbance and frustration. But what does that matter
to us, since the working out in his poetry of whatever
inner conflicts Milton has is amazing realization of dynamic grandeur—grandiosity only in the serio-comic
Battle of the Angels—on a fit subject and occasion?

As if in answer to similar queries, Milton explains that

> God to remove his ways from human sense,
> Placed heaven from earth so far, that earthly sight,
> If it presume, might err in things too high,
> And no advantage gain . . .
>
> *P.L.*, VIII, 119–22

Only at the end of the poem, as solace to his despair, is
Adam in a dream carried up by Michael, who

> from Adam's eyes the film removed
> Which that false fruit that promised clearer sight
> Hath bred; then purged with euphrasy and rue
> The visual nerve, for he had much to see;
> And from the well of life three drops instilled.
>
> *P.L.*, XI, 412–16

In writing his epic Milton relies on the Heavenly
Muse to perform Michael's office. He deliberately pre-
sumes, therefore errs "in things too high," but he does a
superb "advantage gain." Of course he is inescapably of
Satan's party as well as God's, for he could not have
known any of this without having seen, tasted, and in-

wardly digested it. Right instinct causes him to show us
Eden first through Satan's eyes, already contaminated by
his shadow before we can *know* it at all. And if we do
not like Milton's God, there is every reason to believe
that Milton did, that he would have been astonished at
some of our objections, that he found his own beatitude
more real than Dante's.

Meditating during those long years the Fall of man,
weighing the ensuing pain and delight of knowing
through his five senses, God and the world, Milton must
have echoed, with a smile of gratification, St. Augustine's
celebration of the Fall: "O felix culpa!" [12]

[12] What Hegel later called "the fall upward" of course preoccupied
many in the sixteenth and seventeenth centuries besides Milton.

Joyce echoes and re-echoes St. Augustine's cry, usually as "O Phoe-
nix Culprit!" His most direct echo of *Paradise Lost* is of the opening
lines: "Of manifest 'tis obedience and the Flute!" *F.W.,* 343.

II

Creation

"IN THE BEGINNING was the Word, and the Word was with God, and the Word was God." Of Milton's great themes Creation is most completely and serenely realized in his work. It is closest to his heart. He too is an artificer of the word and no other theme offers him such rich correspondence with all he most prizes. For how could he use his own supreme gift more supremely than in celebrating God's great gift of life?

Not yet twenty, Milton writes awkwardly in A Vacation Exercise:

> I have some naked thoughts that rove about
> And loudly knock to have their passage out;

still vaguely but with more fire one of these naked thoughts emerges:

> Such where the deep transported mind may soar
> Above the wheeling poles, and at heaven's door
> Look in, and see each blissful deity
> How he before the thunderous throne doth lie . . .

Then, with growing mastery in his Ode on Christ's Nativity, he first attempts Creation itself:

> Such music (as 'tis said)
> Before was never made,
> But when of old the sons of morning sung,

> While the creator great
> His constellations set,
> And the well-balanced world on hinges hung,
> And cast the dark foundations deep,
> And bid the weltering waves their oozy channel
>   keep.

This same voice attains full timbre and assurance only after years of training and waiting and living, until the Creator, who earlier in artful indirect discourse "bid the weltering waves their oozy channel keep," speaks out with magnificent authority:

> "Silence, ye troubled waves, and thou deep, peace,"
> Said then the omnific word, "your discord end:"
> Nor stayed, but on the wings of cherubim
> Uplifted, in paternal glory rode
> Far into chaos, and the world unborn;
> For chaos heard his voice . . .
>
> P.L., VII, 216–21

Theologians may worry over Milton's shifting conception of the Trinity—why in some passages all Three Persons go forth together, why in these lines God sends Christ forth, why elsewhere the Holy Ghost hatches out the universe. But the Divine creative act is clear, as is its inauguration:

> And thou my word, begotten Son, by thee
> This I perform, speak thou, and be it done:
> My overshadowing spirit and might with thee
> I send along, ride forth, and bid the deep
> Within appointed bounds be heaven and earth.
>
> P.L., VII, 163–67

Christ is the Word. Milton is creating with the word. Of course he explicitly recognizes the difference between any grandeur he can achieve and God's, as well as the limitation of time-bound human speech; yet he unquestionably feels passionate assurance of divine direction when he rides forth, like Christ, to re-create in poetry God's Work.

In this task no other poet has equalled him. Michelangelo alone, when he painted the single section of the Sistine Ceiling which lives up to its superb conception, can compare with Milton's achievement. Dante gives us Hell and Purgatory and Paradise, but only incidentally celebrates the *act* of creation; whereas Milton, though relegating Raphael's story to a single book, never lets us forget from beginning to end the Divine creative process. It is both substance and structure of his epic.

To God, who foresaw and foreknew all at one stroke, Creation is not fulfilled till Adam's final vision of Christ's Coming and Judgment. Without confusing us, Milton makes clear that there are two times in *Paradise Lost*, of far greater significance than the ingenious double-time in *Othello:*

> Immediate are the acts of God, more swift
> Than time or motion, but to human ears
> Cannot without process of speech be told,
> So told as earthly notion can receive.
>
> P.L., VII, 176–79

By deliberately dislocating time sequence, by his mastery of cumulative effects, by his genius for energy and movement in language, he secures the illusion that what is past is still present at the end when all is at last rounded out.

As the poem opens, in our chronology, God looks out

and sees Satan and his host lying prostrate in Hell after the Fall; the world has already been created out of Chaos.[1] But just as Milton keeps always fresh in our minds the physical sense of Satan's fall, "hurled head-long flaming from the ethereal sky," by having his followers constantly recalling it with shuddering terror, by describing it over and over from different points of view —as seen from below in Hell by Sin and Death, from the middle region by Chaos, from above by Raphael, God and his Angels; so, by distributing accounts of Creation in the mouths of various characters—Satan (as rumor), Uriel, Raphael, the chorusing angels, Adam, Eve—he keeps always alive throughout the poem God's continuous creativity.

With the announcement of subject at the opening we are reminded:

> In the beginning how the heavens and earth
> Rose out of chaos,

while the heavenly spirit

> with mighty wings outspread
> Dove-like satest brooding on the vast abyss
> And madest it pregnant.

At the end, after his vision, Adam returns to find new activity:

> for now too nigh
> The archangel stood, and from the other hill
> To their fixed station, all in bright array

[1] *P.L.*, I, 50–58; II, 349; III, 56–76; VII, 131 ff. Action proper begins with Satan's recovery in Hell. The Six Days evidently occur while Satan lies stunned and immobile.

The cherubim descended; on the ground
Gliding meteorous, as evening mist
Risen from a river o'er the marsh glides.
. . . . . . High in front advanced,
The brandished sword of God before them blazed
Fierce as a comet . . .

P.L., XII, 625 ff.

God's never-resting deputies are still at work, this time
closing the gate on Paradise to start that creation of
human history leading to Christ and Judgment—history
which by characteristic dislocation of man's time in an
approximation of God's simultaneity, we have just
experienced.

But Creation is far more deeply interfused in *Paradise
Lost* than these surface devices indicate. Miss Mahood
has brilliantly, if perhaps too ingeniously, demonstrated
how it forms the design and movement of the poem:

> Like the Creator, who, as described in Book VII, be-
> gins His work by setting a compass upon the face of
> the deep, Milton in the opening line of his epic trans-
> fixes the centre of his cosmos—the earth, human life—
> and the nodal point of his action—the Fall of Man. The
> fine Invocation to the Holy Spirit which follows is
> dominated by the idea of flight, and thus prepares us for
> the outward movement of the poet's imagination to-
> wards the circumference, through which he swings the
> other foot of his compasses in the opening words of his
> second paragraph:
>
> > Say first, for Heav'n hides nothing from thy view
> > Nor the deep Tract of Hell . . .
>
> On this circumference, everything is in motion. As a
> natural philosopher, Milton's main objection to the
> Ptolemaic astronomy seems to have been that it postu-

lated an incredible speed in the revolutions of the outer spheres around 'this punctual spot,' the earth. . . . But as a poet, Milton accepted the geocentric universe as the framework to his epic for this very reason that it comprised a still centre and a violently moving periphery.[2]

Miss Mahood demonstrates how the various great shifts in the poem back and forth between Heaven and Earth and Hell parallel the action, the thematic development, the various arcs described by God's compasses —always proceeding from and returning to the focal point, the still and fixed world at the center of this vortex, "with its womb-like security." In her analysis, the main features are outlined by the plunge *in medias res* during the first four books; the formal perfection is revealed by the slow outward and receding movement of the next four; and the last three books serve to restore the symmetry, hitherto flawless, which transgression in the ninth has marred.

Thus the movement of the various actors in this drama, the shifts in focus of attention, the contrasts between motion and rest, sound and silence—all directly enforce the rational meaning to be found in the actors' speeches and Milton's running comment. And by endowing the whole poem with his own amazing sensuous capacity, shared alike by animate and inanimate—even the unformed matter of Chaos, those "embryon atoms" —Milton in his anatomy of the Universe makes all from clod to God one body.

[2] M. M. Mahood, *Poetry and Humanism*, 178 ff. Miss Mahood anticipates my own view so effectively in this respect that it is a privilege to endorse her, with the sole reservation that she tends (in writing of the Fifth, Sixth, Eleventh, Twelfth Books, for instance) to confuse perfection of conception with perfection of execution.

2.

Lessing insists on dividing Time-Space between poetry and painting. Joyce meditates ingeniously throughout *Finnegans Wake* on the Time-Space problem con-
fronting man; to him time is masculine change, space
feminine permanence. But it is Milton who confounds
theory by creating in time a sense of space that remains
unsurpassed even by Dante, who surpasses him in con-
veying mystic union with God, not through sight, hearing, taste, touch, smell, but through the intense light
only of all-pervading love.

To both poets creation is the traditional imposing of
order on chaos; that Milton is magnetically drawn to
Dante's medieval sense of order is clear from his deliberate adaptation of the Ptolemaic system, though he cannot, like Dante, use it without reservation.[3] For this
reason Dante's Hell, Purgatory, Paradise are more precisely calculated in their relation to the earth and each
other than Milton's and more intricately detailed. Nonetheless, we cannot grasp Dante's total scheme without
resort to diagrams, mainly because his urgent desire is
to reach upward to Paradise, in true Platonic-Christian
fashion leaving so far as possible the material senses
behind; his imagery in *Paradiso* sloughs off earth and
water for fire and air. At each stage of his pilgrimage
he puts out of mind the terrain he has passed through.

Milton's fundamental conception of matter as indis-

---

[3] Milton solves this problem simply. Once he has constructed in our
minds his imagined neo-Ptolemaic Universe, he can afford to bring in
the Copernican (*P.L.*, VIII, 122 ff.) on a quibble of Raphael's over-
legitimate and illegitimate knowledge.

tinct from spirit[4] is different, and of course his whole
purpose is different, centered on earth not Paradise,
requiring constant journeying back and forth between
Empyrean and Hell and to all corners of the Universe
in circular progression. Dante, with his detailed traditional map in mind, knows every step of his way. Milton
is his own Mercator, pacing out his map as he progresses
and marking out, as if for the first time, the distances,
the heights, the depths.

Milton's account of actual Creation is postponed till
halfway through the poem, so that we are already familiar with the general outline, the space and its division
into components, the scale, the materials before we
review the process which articulates this order.[5] We have
lain in Hell and explored it; we have with Satan strug-
gled through that unarticulated remnant of primordial
matter in Chaos; we have circled the earthly universe and
entered the Garden; and finally we have climbed with
the Heavenly Muse to the Empyrean, and fallen again
with the Rebellious Angels back to Hell. During all
this time Milton has been impressing on us in manifold
ways the *scale* of Creation, its immensity.

Joyce makes the law of falling bodies—an increase in
velocity of "thirty-two feet per second per second"—in
the figure thirty-two a chief key to his account of man,

---

[4] Dante himself is not always consistent, sometimes considering the
prima materia the direct creation of God, sometimes (*Paradiso*, XIII)
something external acted upon by God and only imperfectly respond-
ing.

[5] To use an analogy from painting, Milton does not move from
finished detail to detail until he is done, but with swift strokes blocks
in broadly the general design; then roughly marks off values of light
and shadow, gradually bringing the whole surface of the canvas simultaneously to completion.

since falling is man's nature. Not so scientifically exact, Milton also repeatedly relies on elapsed time, though he occasionally indicates specific distances. "From the center thrice to the utmost pole" gives a particular distance between Empyrean and the floor of Hell (a distance that we have already fallen six times before we are halfway through the poem). Thus Satan falls thrice the distance from the earth to the *primum mobile* or outer crust of the universe. Voyaging through Chaos in the Second Book, Satan strikes a vacuum and instantly drops a fraction over eleven miles (10,000 fathoms): he would still be falling but for an unlucky updraft of air.

But Milton does not work out his super-Brobdingnagian scheme like Swift in exact figures. These few concessions to human literalness only indicate that all creation is as precisely measurable by God as the fragments within our ken by us. The real sense of the awesome depth of Satan's fall from on high comes from the *time* it took him to fall and to recover from his ensuing daze. Hephaestus when thrown out of Jove's heaven fell a whole summer's day before landing. But as for Satan and his crew, *nine days they fell*. Even if we do not think in terms of thirty-two-feet-per-second every second, we have all acquired in infancy a realistic enough sense of falling speed to grasp the awful implied distance. No wonder the shock of such disaster leaves the heretofore-pain-free Angels unconscious and prostrate

> *Nine times* the *space* that measures day and night.
> P.L., I, 50

Milton here deliberately identifies space and time, just as he speaks of blindness in terms of deafness.

I have already mentioned his extraordinary use of sound and reverberation in building his huge structure. Again and again he dwells on the volume of sound when one-third of these enormous beings who are God's Angels fall in full battle array for nine days to crash on the floor of Hell. And he suggests the time needed for that sound to travel over infinite distance to the ears of Sin, Death, Chaos and old Night, and the time needed for the echoes to bounce back in seemingly endless reverberation. Nor does he neglect the force of displaced air and of the sound waves themselves: if earth had been created then "all earth had to her center shook."

So far we have been considering dimension only. One way Milton causes the heavens and earth to rise out of Chaos with the solidity and form of an actual sphere (as well as vast dimension) is simply by animating Mercator's projection of the earth. This depends on sight and motion. In simplest terms it is movement of the eye as its focus shifts. We come upon it early in the best-known sequence of Milton's similes, which conveys a sense of the superheroic size and multitudinous number of Satan's host, while simultaneously dramatizing their rise from quiescence to vigorous life and movement, from abject defeat to reborn power, and also creates the vault of Hell.

In the First Book Satan floating on the fiery lake "many a rood" is like a vast whale lying off *Norway*. When he moves toward shore his shield is like the moon which Galileo sees at evening from *Fiesole* or in *Valdarno*. His spear dwarfs the tallest pine on *Norwegian* hills. Thus two widely separated geographical points

are established for the two feet of the compass, from
Norway in the north to Italy in the south. And this is
of course only the beginning of a cumulative process.
Satan looks back to see the confusion of his host on the
lake of fire:

> Thick as autumnal leaves that strew the brooks
> In *Vallombrosa*, where the Etrurian shades
> High over arched embower; or scattered sedge
> Afloat, when with fierce winds Orion armed
> Hath vexed the *Red Sea coast*, whose waves o'er-
> threw
> Busiris and his Memphian chivalry . . .
>
> > *P.L.*, I, 302–307

We are again swept with an ease possible only to imagination and dreams from the second focal point, the
Arno river in northern Italy, east and south across the
Mediterranean and Near East to the Red Sea opening
on the Indian Ocean. Those who are map-conscious
(and today for different reasons we are more so than
even the exploring seventeenth century) will feel however faintly a sense of here-to-there section of a globe.
Fifty lines later in another figure we have shifted back
to where the "populous north" pours forth her hordes
to cross

> *Rhene or the Danaw*, when her barbarous sons
> Came like a deluge on the south, and spread
> *Beneath Gibraltar to the Libyan sands*.
>
> > *P.L.*, I, 353–55

This time the arc sweeps from the vast steppes beyond
the Rhine and Danube westward and southward below
Gibraltar, then across the Mediterranean to the Libyan
desert reaching into the heart of Africa.

After thus drawing and quartering Europe and fringes of neighboring Asia and Africa, we are imaginatively prepared for the vastness of Hell with its four great rivers, its frozen and flaming continents. And, lest we think only in terms of length and breadth, we soon receive (*P.L.*, II, 636 ff.) another arc indicating the height of Hell's roof, together with a swift suggestion of the time and effort needed to cover such distance, and the dwarfing of enormous Satan seen afar:

> As when far off at sea a fleet descried
> Hangs in the clouds, by equinoctial winds
> Close sailing *from Bengala, or the isles*
> *Of Ternate and Tidore,* whence merchants bring
> Their spicy drugs: they on the trading flood
> *Through the wide Ethiopian to the cape*
> *Ply stemming nightly toward the pole.*

This time our arc sweeps from the Malay archipelago off East Asia across the Indian Ocean to the southern tip of Africa.

This last figure shows how Milton, having established map-consciousness and space-through-eye movement, adds actual physical movement (both of flying and of sturdily plowing ships) as Satan starts the first of many journeys. Circling with him over the whole universe familiarizes us with the vast locale of the poem, thoroughly explored muscularly with swift ease or laborious difficulty by flying, walking, crawling, wading, swimming, climbing. We are even privileged through Satan's eyes to see the whole world, not just the earth, in relation to Empyrean from outside, shrunk to relative insignificance in the immense cosmos:

And fast by hanging in a golden chain
This pendent world, in bigness as a star
Of smallest magnitude close by the moon.[6]

P.L., II, 1051–53

After we have leaped over an unguarded towering wall into Eden with Satan, lurked there with him in secret to spy on Adam and Eve, been thrown out by Gabriel, the poem shifts point of view for four books. On our return to Satan in the Ninth Book, with that imaginative privilege of poetry to go backward in time, we re-spend those seven intervening days traveling with Satan about the globe—three days circling the earth at the equator from east to west, and four circling from pole to pole (*P.L.*, IX, 63 ff.). In between our parting from Satan and rejoining him we have lived through Raphael's account of God's Six Days. For those vast sweeping arcs described by the Golden Compasses we were amply prepared. Satan's seven-fold circling of the earth, coming just afterwards, continues the persistent circular movement and the spherical form of perfection.

3.

In Milton's Universe nothing is at rest except Heaven, earth, and Hell, and even these are giving forth and receiving influences. All else is moving at various speeds, either in complex harmony like the spheres or violent turbulence like Chaos. The planets are inhaling and exhaling. On earth, land and sea are in ferment. No wonder the poem pulses with life.

---

[6] Milton resorts to double-scale as well as double-time. Here our world is shrunk to a speck; yet Satan falls only one and one half its diameter (*P.L.*, I, 73–74).

Milton's special genius for motion is more easily experienced than explained. It is so marked that Miss Mahood considers him more tactile than oral or aural.[7] Motion is in Milton a kind of sixth sense expressed in imagery, in mimetic rhythms, and by an electric charge which he manages to put into ordinary words, making even nouns, adverbs, adjectives, participles behave like active verbs.[8] This is why kinetic sympathy is aroused by the geographical similes we have just been examining and by Satan's busy travels, as

> He *scours* the right hand coast, sometimes the left.
> Now *shaves with level wing* the deep, then *soars* . . .
>
> P.L., II, 633–34

Neither Satan nor any of the other angels tamely fly from here to there. Each flight has its special quality, often its particular angle. Instinctively the flyer seems to test air resistance, seek or avoid air currents. We always know the state of the atmosphere—whether the pure serene of upper regions or the density of lower—as well as the state of mind and purpose, registered by leisurely coasting or meteor speed. An angel can *spring upward like a pyramid of fire, glide* like Uriel on a sunbeam "swift as a shooting star," *throw his steep flight in*

[7] M. M. Mahood, *Poetry and Humanism*, 201. This is a refreshing change from regarding Milton as predominantly aural; but we have already seen how misleading it is to concentrate on any single sense with Milton.

[8] Milton's great fondness for Latinisms, far from being pedantry, is largely explained by their active literal meanings. *Insult*, for example, is literally *to leap on* or *at*; *tempt* is *to handle, touch*. D. C. Allen (*The Harmonious Vision*, 107) remarks: "It is not only Satan who is made visible by motion; whole scenes are made flesh *by this forceful use of verbs*."

many an airy wheel, stoop like a down-swooping hawk.
Milton himself, we remember, *soars* over the Olympian
hill "above the flight of Pegasean wing," and all these
fantasies of flight during his blindness must have been
based on earlier close observation of birds as well as
knowledge of natural laws. In each instance the rhythm
of the verse helps convey the quality of flight, yet it is
hardly more responsible than the nice calculation of
effort needed to form the words chosen.

As no one tamely flies no one simply falls. Even in a
passing allusion to Mulciber-Hephaestus the quality of
the human body as a projectile is there. First he is flung
sailing in a wide arc:

> From heaven, they fabled, thrown by angry Jove
> *Sheer o'er the crystal battlements:*

then inexorably he turns straight downward with the
fascination of slow motion:

> from morn
> To noon he fell, from noon to dewy eve,
> A summer's day;

but he gathers speed, just as the sun, so long sinking
in the west, draws close to the horizon and suddenly
drops below:

> and with the setting sun
> *Dropped from the zenith like a falling star*
> On Lemnos the Aegaean isle . . .
>
> P.L., I, 741–46

The whole violence of Satan's more terrible fall is in the
phrase *hurled headlong,* requiring for its utterance violent expulsion of breath; then comes the turn in air:

flaming from the ethereal sky, the quickening rhythm; *with hideous ruin and combustion down.* The sense of falling is conveyed by our *making,* not just hearing, the sounds and rhythms.

Cited often for metrical daring are three lines which are more justly famous for their varying quality of effort and motion. The fiend, eager as a thief escaping with the loot,

> O'er bog or steep, through strait, rough, dense, or rare,
> With head, hands, wings or feet pursues his way,
> And swims or sinks, or wades, or creeps, or flies . . .
> *P.L.,* II, 948–50

At the other extreme is the magical ease with which Pandemonium, that fabulously huge edifice, *rose like an exhalation.*

The sun rarely *shines* in Milton. He *impresses his beams* or *smites* or *gently penetrates.* And earth may be the stationary center of this wheeling universe, but it is fermenting with its own life and motion. Streams by a kind of osmosis

> through veins
> Of porous earth with kindly thirst updrawn
> *P.L.,* IV, 227–28

spring into fountains. Satan recoils from Abdiel's stroke,

> as if on earth
> Winds under ground or waters forcing way
> Sidelong, had pushed a mountain from his seat
> Half-sunk with all his pines.
> *P.L.,* VI., 195–98

The terrain of Hell is such

                        as when the force
        Of subterranean wind transports a hill
        Torn from Pelorus, or the shattered side
        Of thundering Etna, whose combustible
        And fueled entrails thence conceiving fire,
        Sublimed with mineral fury, aid the winds . . .
                                    P.L., I, 230 ff.

To convey terrific energy Milton taps all the natural
and cosmic sources he can think of—volcano, earth-
quake, comet, planetary collision, explosion. Satan when
discovered by Ithuriel does not merely change from
disguise back to his proper likeness; he *explodes* from
toad to angel:

                        As when a spark
        Lights on a heap of nitrous powder, laid
        Fit for the tun some magazine to store
        Against a rumored war, the smutty grain
        With sudden blaze diffused, inflames the air:
        So started up in his own shape the fiend.
                                    P.L., IV, 814–19

Menaced by Death, Satan kindles like a comet; the
threatened encounter between the two is that of thun-
derheads. Angels in the Battle of Heaven in their cata-
clysmic impact are colliding planets.

    Motion Milton identifies with life itself. Some of his
creatures cannot wait to be fully born before displaying
energy. The waters flow together and at once the dol-
phins play, Leviathan "draws in and at his trunk spouts
out the sea." Trees rise *dancing* like the Pleiades.

            The grassy clods now calved, now half appeared
            The tawny lion, *pawing to get free*
            His hinder parts, then springs as broke from bonds,
            And rampant shakes his brindled mane; the ounce,

The libbard, and the tiger, as the mole
Rising, the crumbled earth above them threw
In hillocks . . . *scarce from his mold*
Behemoth biggest born of earth *upheaved*
His vastness . . .

P.L., VII, 463 ff.

Adam has hardly opened his eyes when "raised by quick instinctive motion" he springs erect.

"The grassy clods now *calved*" is significant. Geography, astronomy, meteorology, geometry, dynamics—all these serve merely to describe not explain this vital energy. These purely masculine abstractions—even the superb Golden Compasses drawing the circle of perfection—have done all they can to conceive and project the mystery. Adam remains inert in all his symmetry till God breathes in his nostrils the breath of life. He is ineffectual till God gives him "female for race." Milton has already admitted through the back door at the very beginning the animating principle which Raphael admits only obliquely:

and other suns perhaps
With their attendant moons thou wilt descry
Communicating male and female light,
Which two great sexes animate the world.

P.L., VIII, 148–51

4.

This pregnant admission of Raphael's comes at the end of his account of the Six Days of Creation. Only in connection with the moon, with her mysterious power over tides and women, is light ever female in Milton. Elsewhere it is always male, as his larger symbolism in which God is Light, requires. On the First Day comes the authoritative Word, "Let there be light," and, already in existence, the "co-eternal beam" springs from the deep to be the generating principle of all life.

"Female light" [9] reveals a difficulty Milton has in elaborating the simple thread of the Genesis story which he so punctiliously follows. He has somehow to introduce a female element into a purely masculine cosmic scheme. He discards with a few glancing allusions the cabalistic sephiroth,[10] with which he was familiar, probably for essential simplicity and with the conviction that it is no concern of his to explain more than is explained in Genesis.

Raphael's various speculations with Adam in the Eighth Book admit without resolving these difficulties. However the female element got into the Universe before the creation of Eve, from the start two great sexes animate the world. In the universe within Adam's ken the sun is the source of light and the fertilizing agent. Raphael in his additional revelations stresses an obvious

[9] Of course, that the female moon's paler light is mere reflection of the sun's fits neatly Milton's belief in subordination of woman to man—"He for God only, she for God in him." But this secondary symbolism conflicts with and confuses the primary.

[10] According to the cabalists, when unmanifest God becomes manifest in the Son, the Knower, the Holy Ghost expresses this relationship between knower and known. God Himself is the creator of this Heavenly Trinity, the first 3 numbers in the decade. Then the Son creates the trinity of Man (Word made flesh), the Holy Ghost the trinity of the physical world. These three trinities make up the number 9 and represent the masculine aspects of God. But none of these becomes *living form* until received into the womb of the feminine aspect, represented by 0. Thus we arrive at completion of the decade with 10, which is incidentally a combination of masculine 1 and feminine 0. This scheme assumes that God is bisexual, which Joyce accepts but Milton does not, ignoring also the hint of bisexuality in Plato. (For this brief summary I am indebted to J. C. Campbell and H. M. Robinson, *A Skeleton Key to Finnegans Wake*, 193–95.)

fundamental fact: without the "deep" or the earth the sun is sterile:

> Whose virtue on itself works no effect,
> But in the fruitful earth; there first received
> His beams, unactive else, their vigor find.
>
> P.L., VIII, 95–97

When we come to Satan we shall discover how this sterility can manifest itself in naked aggression. But before Satan's advent in Adam's universe all light shares this fertilizing function—even the faint stars to the extent of fomenting, nourishing, warming, shedding down

> Their stellar virtue on all kinds that grow
> On earth, made hereby *apter to receive*
> *Perfection from the sun's more potent ray.*
>
> P.L., IV, 671–73

We have already seen how the rising sun shoots down his rays to "warm earth's inmost womb" (*P.L.*, V, 300 ff.), and to each inward part of the whole universe

> With gentle penetration, though unseen,
> Shoots invisible virtue even to the deep.
>
> P.L., III, 585–86

These key passages are as much uterine as phallic.

The boldness and candor of this physiological comment and imagery show the untroubled, unembarrassed acceptance of sex without which Milton could convey neither his imaginatively convincing picture of innocence between man and woman nor vitality in Creation. So full-blooded a poet as Milton, so passionate a vitalist, could not help pouring enormous sexual energy into *Paradise Lost*, both consciously and unconsciously. This does not in the slightest impair his deep reverence. His view of sex is one with his view of God, all facets of whose creation he finds good. While leaving unmistakable the physical relation between Adam and Eve, he relegates this sexual imagery to the surrounding universe to vigorously express God's generative abundance.

If Milton cannot rival Dante's sense of mystic union in God's love, he portrays better than Dante God's joy in abundance. Never before or since was such plenitude as when at the moment of Creation God says to Christ:

> Boundless the deep, because *I am who fill*
> *Infinitude*, nor vacuous the space.
>
> P.L., VII, 168–69

And it is this plenitude boldly expressed which vitalizes what would otherwise be only a geometrically-perfect deistic machine whirling through its mechanical rounds. Toward the end Michael still once more reminds Adam that God's

> omnipresence fills
> Land, sea, and air, and every kind that lives,
> *Fomented by his virtual power and warmed.*
>
> P.L., XI, 336–38

Milton has fused them so skilfully that we do not at first realize he is using two distinct methods in dramatizing Creation, two different sets of images and symbols: abstract and concrete, spirit and matter, mind and body, the spontaneous existence as if by magic with the spoken word and natural biological evolution through time. Both methods are in the opening paragraph of the poem, where, as if by a power inherent in the words as they are voiced

> heavens and earth
> Rose out of chaos;

whereas a moment later we find that the heavenly spirit for an indeterminate period

> Dove-like satest brooding on the vast abyss
> And madest it pregnant.

Thus Milton, long before Raphael stresses them, tacitly accepts the "two great sexes" animating the world. By passing constantly from one method and one set of symbols to the other he manages to infuse this brooding warmth into his abstractions, so that when we come to the Golden Compasses drawing swift arcs over Chaos the image seems more biological than geometric. Without Milton's committing himself metaphysically, matter is to all intents and purposes the feminine aspect of God. In his immensely effective and yet simple account of the Six Days, this earthly universe is born of the brooding spirit from the "womb of unoriginal night and chaos wild":[11]

> Darkness profound
> Covered the abyss: but on the watery calm
> His brooding wings the spirit of God outspread,
> And vital virtue infused, and vital warmth
> Throughout the fluid mass . . .
>
> P.L., VII, 233 ff.

Then with no confusion Milton shifts to the other method. Light is summoned forth, divided into day and night, parceled out to sun, moon, stars by a divine magic

[11] This phrase I have transposed from a quite different context (P.L., X, 476–77) where it is threatening—a seeming contradiction which I shall consider later.

which even in the poem (as in Michelangelo's greatest panel—creation of sun and moon) makes it seem to come into being as its name is uttered.

But earth does not rise like an exhalation. However miraculous, the creation of earth combines the two methods, beginning with biological, time-consuming birth:

> The earth was formed, but in the womb as yet
> Of waters, embryon immature involved,
> Appeared not: over all the face of earth
> Main ocean flowed, not idle, but with warm
> Prolific humor softening all her globe,
> Fermented the great mother to conceive,
> Satiate with genial moisture,

then the wizard voice:

>   when God said
> "Be gathered now ye waters under heaven
> Into one place, and let dry land appear."
> Immediately the mountains huge appear
> Emergent, and their broad bare backs upheave
> Into the clouds . . .
>
>   *P.L.*, VII, 276 ff.

And so in this extraordinary combination of magician's wand and homely birth the Six Days pass, with their evening rests and musical intervals initiating the music of the spheres, until the great angelic hymn on the Seventh:

> "Open, ye everlasting gates," they sung,
> "Open, ye heavens, your living doors; let in
> The great Creator from his work returned
> Magnificent, his six days' work, a world . . .
>
>   *P.L.*, VII, 565 ff.

The Seventh is the day of rest, "but not in silence holy kept." Characteristically Miltonic and unpuritanically Puritan is the celestial Sabbath, with its blazing gold, heavenly music of instruments and voice, clouds of incense fuming from golden censers—all to delight eye, ear, nose. This *Gloria* of the angelic choir echoes at its close the command of plentitude which God has laid in turn on sea, on land, on humankind:

> And multiply a race of worshipers
> Holy and just: thrice happy if they know
> Their happiness.
>
> *P.L.*, VII, 630–32

Against this emergent cosmos of unspeakable grandeur Milton must place without too much disparity the human couple. This disproportion is the most serious problem in the entire epic; but at the opening of the Eighth Book the shift in scale is easy, partly because Milton focuses the attention of the angelic choir on man's entrance and also returns to Raphael, the narrator whom we have completely forgotten during his narrative; mainly because this is the familiar transition in the second chapter of Genesis, which Milton follows almost word for word, with some help from Job and the Psalms (and of course the hexaemeral tradition). After the symphonic grandeur of the Seventh Book, Adam's own story is like a solo on a reed instrument; nonetheless, it is simply another variation on the same theme of creation and plenitude.

Quickening personal interest compensates for abrupt shift in scale, for this is our own ancestral experience. Significantly, Adam's recollection is nothing more than

the original awakening of the senses: first *touch*, as he
becomes aware of the soft flowery grass on which he
lies and the feel of the warm sun evaporating his "balmy
sweat"; then *sight*, as his gaze is at once drawn *upward*
to the ample heaven; then *motion*, as instinctively he
springs erect; then *sound* and *smell* (the senses soon
begin their normal coalescence), as he hears birdsong
and discovers that "all things smiled with fragrance."
Taste comes last, in his dream, when prophetically the
fruit

> that hung to the eye
> Tempting, stirred in me sudden appetite
> To pluck and eat.
>
> P.L., VIII, 307–309

Yet his first oral manifestation, typically, is not eating
but speech. After scrutinizing himself limb by limb,
Adam recognizes instinctively the life force, *light* of the
sun and *enlightened* earth, almost as if he had heard the
last words of the angelic choir singing: "Thrice happy if
they know their happiness:"

> Tell me, how may I know him, how adore,
> From whom I have that thus I move and live,
> And feel that I am happier than I know.
>
> P.L., VIII, 280–82

In Genesis, after commanding Adam not to eat of the
tree of knowledge, God remarks at once: *It is not good
that man should be alone; I will make him an help
meet for him.* From this text Milton departs slightly.
His Adam, after naming the beasts of the field and seeing
their inferiority, before God has time to divulge further
plans, recognizes his own loneliness and incompleteness.

Further, Adam boldly ventures even to dispute with God on the questions of equality and Unity in Trinity. Having lost the seventeenth century passion for disputation, we find God's pleasure in Adam's sudden suspiciously-Arian argumentative skill faintly humorous, like a father with a precocious child. But Milton departs from Genesis deliberately to stress an essential point of his creed: God creates man with independent God-like reason which awakens as naturally as his senses and at the same time. Rousseau's Instinctive Innocent has blurred for us Milton's (Augustinian) Intellectual Innocent.

Adam takes Eve with thanksgiving but in the spirit of an Old Testament patriarch, almost as a vassal. If this now discredited seventeenth-century view of woman alienates modern readers, it makes all the more poignant Adam's eloquent tribute to Eve, his "mysterious reverence" for the "genial bed." [12] Immediately the verse takes on the lyrical quality of epithalamion and a Tennysonian lilt:

> To the nuptial bower
> I led her blushing like the morn: all heaven,
> And happy constellations on that hour
> Shed their selectest influence; the earth
> Gave signs of gratulation, and each hill;
> *Joyous the birds; fresh gales and gentle airs*
> *Whispered it to the woods, and from their wings*
> *Flung rose, flung odors from the spicy shrub,*
> Disporting, till the amorous bird of night
> Sung spousal, and bid haste the evening star
> On his hilltop to light the bridal lamp.
>
> P.L., VIII, 510–20

[12] As usual, Milton intends not only the secondary meaning, *festive*, but the primary meaning of *genial—pertaining to generation.*

"Transported touch" indeed sweeps Adam from Reason's mooring. He reminds himself of woman's inferiority of mind and spirit, her slighter resemblance to the Divine Image (being a copy of a copy), yet wonders if perhaps God in creating her did not take more than a rib from his side:

> yet when I approach
> Her loveliness, so absolute she *seems*
> And in herself complete, so well to know
> Her own, that what she wills to do or say,
> *Seems* wisest, virtuousest, discreetest, best;
> All higher knowledge in her presence falls
> Degraded, wisdom in discourse with her
> Loses discountenanced, and like folly shows:
> *Authority and reason on her wait,*
> *As one intended first, not after made*
> *Occasionally*; and to consummate all,
> Greatness of mind and nobleness their seat
> Build in her loveliest, and create an awe
> About her, as a guard angelic placed.
>
> P.L., VIII, 546–59

Woman has seldom received higher praise, even when we discount Milton's intent to foreshadow, so soon after Eve's creation, the passion which will shortly cause Adam's downfall, and after him Samson's. She *seems* complete in herself; he *knows* she is complete only in him. Raphael with a frown reproves this excess, this abdication of the male, warning Adam: "Be not diffident." Surprisingly, diffidence lies behind much of Milton's aggressive masculinity.[13]

[13] When only a callow twenty-two, in one of his Italian sonnets (Moody's translation) Milton writes:

> Lady, the humble offering of my heart
> To you I dedicate: be sure, in many trials

And they were both naked, the man and his wife, and were not ashamed. This verse in Genesis Milton develops with exultation and contempt for "these troublesome disguises which we wear." Having already surrounded with rich imagery of generation the universe which Adam and Eve inhabit, he has only to gather them silently into the rhythm of plenitude, so that they seem, till eating the forbidden fruit, never self-conscious, each aware only of the other and of sharing in a general process of nature. Except, as we have just noticed, Adam is already beginning to worry over his passionate transport; and Eve we soon find restless for more privacy. It is not long till both are ripe for Satan.

For the most part Milton serenely accepts the beauty of this naked love, but once or twice his tone, not Adam's and Eve's behavior, is aggressive:

> Straight side by side were laid, nor turned I ween
> Adam from his fair spouse, nor Eve the rites
> Mysterious of connubial love refused:
> Whatever hypocrites austerely talk
> Of purity and place and innocence,
> Defaming as impure what God declares
> Pure, and commands to some, leaves free to all.
> Our maker bids increase, who bids abstain
> But our destroyer, foe to God and man?
>
> P.L., IV, 741–49

The ancient doctrine of plenitude, which Chaucer, Shakespeare, Spenser accept as a matter of course, Mil-

---

I found it faithful, constant, valorous,
Gracious of thought, discreet, and good.

.   .   .   .

In one sole part *thou'lt find it not so strong*
Where Love set his incurable sting.

ton has to defend against a new conspiracy of silence. With none of the hesitation of St. Paul, Raphael on entering Eden greets Eve:

> Hail mother of mankind, whose fruitful womb
> Shall fill the world more numerous with thy sons
> Than with these various fruits the trees of God
> Have heaped this table.
>
> P.L., V, 388–91

The unself-conscious purity of these marital relations in Paradise, difficult to render at best, sometimes a little bruised by Milton's belligerence, is perhaps most apparent in casual moments like Adam's awakening to feast his eyes on Eve in a fashion so different from Satan's voyeurism:

> he on his side
> Leaning half raised, with looks of cordial love
> Hung over her enamored, and beheld
> Beauty, which whether waking or asleep,
> Shot forth peculiar graces . . .
>
> P.L., V, 11–15

But Eve herself had not slept well, her hair is disarranged, her face is flushed. Satan has already got to her in a dream. Knowing the insuperable problem of portraying purity that is sensuous and full-blooded, Milton wisely cuts short the state of absolute innocence before Satan enters and by his presence in the Garden at once touches it with incipient decay.

All things considered, Milton succeeds remarkably in giving an illusion of innocence, of the unknowable. When we question some of Adam's knowledgeable conversations with Eve before he has been instructed by Raphael, we must remember that Milton not only has to transpose into our vocabulary what presumably they said, but also that not till a later generation was the human mind considered a *tabula rasa* at birth. Original Sin in ourselves explains why our Great Parents do not come fully alive for us until they are tempted and fall.

Adam, our true father, cannot bear to let Raphael go without satisfying one final curiosity. How do the angels express their love:

> by looks only, or do they mix
> Irradiance, virtual or immediate touch?

Raphael smiles a "celestial rosy red, love's proper hue" and answers Adam as he and Eve might answer us:

> Let it suffice thee that thou knowest
> Us happy, and without love no happiness.
> Whatever pure thou in the body enjoyest
> (And pure thou wert created) we enjoy
> In eminence, and obstacle find none
> Of membrane, joint, or limb, exclusive bars . . .
> P.L., VIII, 616 ff.

5.

Such bliss was Archangel Satan's till his rebellious mind gave birth full-grown to Sin, whom he first despised, then loved too well:

> and such joy thou tookest
> With me in secret, that my womb conceived
> A growing burden.
> P.L., II, 765–67

This time birth, as recounted by Sin, is hideous travesty of plenitude:

                        my womb
Pregnant by thee, and now excessive grown
Prodigious motion felt and rueful throes.
At last this odious offspring whom thou seest
Thine own begotten, breaking violent way
Tore through my entrails, that with fear and pain
Distorted, all my nether shape thus grew
Transformed: but he my inbred enemy
Forth issued, brandishing his fatal dart
Made to destroy: I fled and cried out "Death;"
Hell trembled at the hideous name, and sighed
From all her caves, and back resounded "Death."
I fled, but he pursued (though more, it seems,
Inflamed with lust than rage) and swifter far,
Me overtook his mother all dismayed,
And in embraces forcible and foul
Engendering with me, of that rape begot
These yelling monsters that with ceaseless cry
Surround me, as thou sawest, hourly conceived
And hourly born, with sorrow infinite
To me, for when they list into the womb
That bred them they return, and howl and gnaw
My bowels, their repast . . .

                                    P.L., II, 778 ff.

Nothing in the whole poem stuns us more with the
impact of the fall than this monstrous transformation of
love into double incest, rape, cannibalism, fearful deformity.[14] And as Satan goes about the universe, tar-

___

[14] That this whole passage is allegory heightens rather than diminishes
its powerful imaginative effect. Even our best critics are still uneasy
about allegory. D. C. Allen, *The Harmonious Vision*, 24, deplores
any hint of "didactic allegory" in considering *Comus*. And Arnold
Stein, *Answerable Style*, 158, in the midst of a beautifully sensitive
passage refers to "the *crude* mechanistic existence of allegorical being,"
making an oversubtle point of the shift from naturalism to allegory,
familiar to Milton from Spenser's constant usage.

nished but still magnificent, he carries with him this horrible secret of his own progeny in Hell, nor can we exorcize them from memory. Generation degenerates. Womb of life becomes womb of death, explaining perhaps why unconsciously Milton uses this image so often to express the prime fear of creation-reversed which haunts the Fallen Angels, most eloquently voiced by Belial:

> To perish rather, swallowed up and lost
> In the wide womb of uncreated night,
> Devoid of sense and motion . . .
>
> P.L., II, 149–51

We are not surprised to find that erasing *sense* and *motion* is Milton's way of expressing oblivion.

Generation is transformed in another, less spectacular but equally deadly way; for all is balance in Milton. Fertility of sun and earth, not limited to animal and vegetable, on which the sun *impresses his beams* as Jupiter *impregns the clouds,* carries even to the geological deep. Satan's devilish ingenuity occasions another arresting birth passage:

> Deep under ground, materials dark and crude,
> Of spiritous and fiery spume, *till touched*
> *With heaven's ray,* and tempered they shoot forth
> So beauteous, opening to the ambient light.
> *These in their dark nativity the deep*
> *Shall yield us pregnant with infernal flame.*

So far the familiar natural creative process. Then Satan perverts with "creation" of his own—artillery:

> Which into hollow engines long and round
> Thick-rammed, at the other bore with touch of fire

Dilated and infuriate shall send forth
From far with thundering noise among our foes . . .
> *P.L.*, VI, 478–87

The female element drops out. The male becomes lethal like the womb of death. In general throughout *Paradise Lost,* whenever the imagery and symbolism are exclusively tumid or tumescent, we find naked aggression and rebellion: all those *horrent arms, rigid spears bristling with upright beams innumerable,* Death's *dreadful dart,* as he menaces Satan:

> and in shape,
> So speaking and so threatening, grew tenfold
> More dreadful and deform:
>> *P.L.*, II, 704–706

And Satan himself defiantly facing the angelic squadron,

> Collecting all his might dilated stood,
> Like Teneriff or Atlas unremoved:
> His stature reached the sky, and on his crest
> Sat horror plumed . . .
>> *P.L.*, IV, 986–89

Part of the Fifth and all of the Sixth Books are given over to braying discord, open hostility, aggression without quarter asked or received, in which God through Christ Militant in the terrible splendors of Ezekiel takes grim part.

The father-symbol is destructive as well as creative, as first Satan, then Adam finds when "that golden scepter" turns to "an iron rod to bruise and break" (*P.L.*, V, 886–88). That destruction is an essential complement of creation is God's mystery, which Milton can portray but not explain. Clearly Satan's defection initiates another phase of creativity.

Satan plots against God and at the very instant of plotting begins to corrupt all he touches. Love at once becomes lust. Serene, untroubled generation yields to sexual guilt and fear, as if Satan's own sin were a decomposing body dropped into a pool, spreading ever wider circles of scum over the clear waters of Creation. Foreseeing this, God simultaneously with Satan's defection creates a world in Hell opposite to that of Eden, which eventually it contaminates:

> A universe of death, which God by curse
> Created evil, for evil only good,
> Where all life dies, death lives, and nature breeds,
> Perverse, all monstrous, all prodigious things,
> Abominable, inutterable, and worse
> Than fables yet have feigned, or fear conceived,
> Gorgons and hydras, and chimeras dire.
>
> P.L., II, 622–28

Here is the sum of mankind's nightmares. In this region of polymorphous perverse, so terrible that Milton only hints it, sex becomes unclean, terrifying, threatening yet compulsive. Here at the nether end of the Universe whose very soul is order and shapeliness we meet "on either side a formidable shape." Male and female—so beautiful in their harmonious interaction in Empyrean Heaven, in sun and earth, in Adam and Eve—are transformed to the ultimate horror:

> The one *seemed* woman to the waist, and fair,
> But ended foul in many a scaly fold
> Voluminous and vast, a serpent armed
> With mortal sting: about her middle round

A cry of hell hounds never ceasing barked
With wide Cerberean mouths full loud, and rung
A hideous peal; yet, when they list, would creep,
If aught disturbed their noise, into her womb,
And kennel there . . . Far less abhorred than these
Vexed Scylla bathing in the sea . . .
Nor uglier follow the night-hag, when called
In secret, riding through the air she comes
Lured with the smell of infant blood . . .

And together with her

> The other shape,
> *If shape it might be called that shape had none*
> Distinguishable in member, joint, or limb.
> . . . . . . black it stood as night,
> Fierce as ten furies, terrible as hell,
> And shook a dreadful dart; what seemed his head
> The likeness of a kingly crown had on.
>
> P.L., II, 650 ff.

Furthermore, to heap horror on horror's head Milton takes advantage of the patristic notion that the Fallen Angels afterwards become heathen gods; he pours on them all the ancient prophets' distilled hatred of the idolatrous and lewd practices which again and again seduced the Children of Israel from God—the "lustful orgies" enlarged under Solomon even to "that hill of scandal." In particular two among Satan's followers are symbols of spiritual rather than physical disgust, projections of Satan's depravity without relief of any virtue:

> Belial the dissolutest spirit that fell,
> The sensualest, and after Asmodai
> The fleshliest incubus . . .
>
> P.R., II, 150–52

Asmodeus' unbridled lust for Sarah causes him to murder in turn seven husbands before he is driven off.[15] Unlike Satan, Belial loves vice for itself: "a spirit more lewd fell not from heaven"; one whose altar is in no special place but wherever lust and violence reign in the hearts of men:

> And when night
> Darkens the streets, then wander forth the sons
> Of Belial, flown with insolence and wine.
> Witness the streets of Sodom, and that night
> In Gibeah, when the hospitable door
> Exposed a matron to avoid worse rape.
>
> P.L., I, 500–505

To rape, incest, abortive deformity are added the special vices of Sodom and Gomorrah.[16] But Sodom and Gomorrah, so prominent in Proust's portrait of social decay, which Joyce in turn transforms into the tragi-comedy of infant chatter about those "bad pities of the plain" (F.W., 564), are in Milton's nightmare only incidental to the monstrous distortions of normal sex in the classic human crime—incest, doubled in Satan and Sin, Sin and Death.

All this imagery of fear and horror follows everywhere close on the heels of Satan, who cannot obliterate what he has called into being in the Universe. Like Macbeth, he is "in blood stepped in so far" that to return would be as difficult as to go on. Throttling his fears and

---

[15] A favorite allusion of Milton's to the Book of Tobit: P.L., IV, 168; V, 221; VI, 365; P.R., II, 151.

[16] Another reference is found in Satan's account of Tiberius' "horrid lust," P.R., IV, 90; and there is a faint suggestion in the "tall stripling youths"—Ganymede and Hylas—in P.R., II, 352–53.

doubts, he accomplishes his mission, as he is careful to boast on his return to Hell:

> Long were to tell
> What I have done, what suffered, with what pain
> Voyaged the unreal, vast, unbounded deep
> Of horrible confusion . . . . . but I
> Toiled out my uncouth passage, forced to ride
> The untractable abyss, plunged in the womb
> Of unoriginal night and chaos wild . . .
>
> P.L., X, 469 ff.

But in the great Generative Process Satan is more than a link in the chain leading to Death and all this world of formless horrors. He is part of the force coming into being when God changes from static to dynamic. At first glance he seems even to initiate the creation of man, since by depleting the angelic hosts he causes God to create the new race and new world. Yet movement actually starts when God decides to become manifest in the Trinity. In his account Milton *assumes* this initial phase of creation, thus avoiding many theological commitments, and begins with the elevation of pre-existent Christ, which crystallizes Satan's dissatisfaction into open action and precipitates creation, fall, and redemption of mankind.[17]

Once started—partly because it has to be transposed into human terms to be comprehensible—the drama seems to vibrate between a polarity of good and evil, to be a cosmic contest in which God finally through Christ

[17] No other epic can equal the beautifully articulated simplicity of Milton's double plot, in which the fall of man not only parallels the fall of Satan but is caused by it, and is redeemed by Christ, the cause of Satan's fall.

checkmates Satan, the Adversary. Yet whatever else he is, Milton is no Manichean dualist. Everything, including Satan, is one with God. On the First Day, before summoning Light into action, the spirit of God infuses warm virtue into the fluid mass:

> *but downward purged*
> *The black tartareous cold infernal dregs*
> *Adverse to life . . . . .*
>
> P.L., VII, 237–39

These "infernal dregs adverse to life" are not obliterated but merely pushed down into Hell and dark pockets in the Universe of Light. With them, though born himself of light, Satan has affinity. With his penetration into Eden, they rise again to our world. He wins over Eve, then Adam, because he already has an ally within the gates, for they too have an affinity with the dregs adverse to life. In making Creation a continuous process—not just placing man in static innocence—Milton must recognize and justify these disparate elements.

While dramatizing an essential process in human development and relation to God, Satan also in a deeply reverent poem drains off harmlessly these natural antithetic and anti-social drives: self-love, pride, envy, hatred, frustration, unbridled desire, all lusts of the ego, together with their nightmare fear and guilt. Through him, after doing his best with God's reasoning on unfathomable mysteries, Milton, without fear of being struck by divine wrath, can speak back all the doubts, the violent objections to things as they are. With Milton we go through the ritual-release of damning ourselves in Satan, yet admiring what we damn, since he is essential to the only cycle of being we know—life-death-life—to which even God, become Man in Christ, submits.

We have seen how effectively in concrete imagery Milton brings home to us the consequences of Satan's fall, disrupting but not destroying God's plenitude. What of his first revolt, which Milton makes the biological as well as spiritual conception of Sin? Essentially it is of course rebellion against authority brought to a head by God's elevating Christ to the Trinity. Before that, Satan's attitude toward God seems to have been ambivalent yet restrained.

In essence what is this but a law of life, the eternal need of the son to supplant the father, to deny authority? Gabriel strips bare Satan's heroic pretensions:

> And thou sly hypocrite, who now wouldst seem
> Patron of liberty, who more than thou
> Once fawned, and cringed, and servilely adored
> Heaven's awful monarch? wherefore but in hope
> To dispossess him, and thyself to reign?
>
> *P.L.*, IV, 957–61

Later Abdiel warns him, trying to avert inevitable disaster:

> *As by his word the mighty father made*
> *All things, even thee* . . . . . .
> . . . . Cease then this impious rage,
> And tempt not these: but hasten to appease
> The incensed father, and the incensed Son
> While pardon may be found in time besought . . .
>
> *P.L.*, V, 836 ff.

But by now Satan's reckless, no-longer-restrained ego insanely denies the Father, as we in solipsism deny, yet at the same time affirm, Creation each time we sin in thought or deed:

> who saw
> When this creation was? rememberest thou
> Thy making, while the maker gave thee being?
> We know no time when we were not as now;
> Know none before us, *self-begot, self-raised*
> *By our own quickening power* . . .
>
> P.L., V, 856–61

With this denial promptly the precarious ambivalence, love-hate, is split. Hate is loosed upon the world. Envious of God's authority, jealous of Christ and later of Adam, the new favorite, henceforth Satan is given over to fraud and malice, determined to destroy man at whatever cost to himself. Worst of all, in suicidal rage and despair Satan curses the sun, the light, symbol supreme of love and life:

> O thou that with surpassing glory crowned,
> Lookest from thy sole dominion like the god
> Of this new world: at whose sight all the stars
> Hide their diminished heads; to thee I call,
> But with no friendly voice, and add thy name
> O sun, to tell thee how *I hate thy beams* . . .
>
> P.L., IV, 32 ff.

That this whole speech is cast in the form of self-searching dramatic soliloquy was early noted by Phillips; these first-composed lines epitomize Satan in what was to become the central symbolism of the poem as light-murderer. Satan's theme is announced a dozen lines earlier: "Now conscience wakes despair." Furthermore, the speech is filled with echoes of that earlier drama of

damnation, Marlowe's *Doctor Faustus*, and brings into
the open what the imagery has already conveyed:

> for within him hell
> He brings, and round about him, nor from hell
> One step no more than from himself can fly . . .
>
> *P.L.*, IV, 20–22

Satan, who has many functions in the poem—personifi-
cation, scapegoat, lightning rod, champion—is here completely humanized in the most awesome of tragedies: a
man facing damnation of his soul. It is impossible not
to feel for him as we feel for Faustus and for Saul, from
whom God likewise turns away His face and His mercy.

Heretofore, though Milton has already made clear a
planned deterioration, Satan has been a magnificent
hero-villain, brilliantly endowed in mind and heart and
body, more human in his super-humanity than Milton
dares to make God.[18] For when in the poem does God
feel the compassion which makes Satan at one point
speechless?

> Thrice he essayed, and thrice in spite of scorn,
> Tears such as angels weep, burst forth . . .
>
> *P.L.*, I, 619–20

At creation Satan, like Adam after him, is endowed with
the reason which enables him to dispute with God Him-

---

[18] To the extent that Satan is a dramatic characterization (which he
is not consistently), Milton shows the influence of Marlowe, Shakespeare, and Jacobean drama. On a few occasions, as during the Battle
in Heaven, Milton endows Satan with a somewhat debatable sense of
humor. But the attempt of Charles Williams and C. S. Lewis to turn
him into a figure of farce is the fault more of their own boredom and
lack of sympathy with Milton than Milton's lapse. Lewis, too, argues
usually from a strongly held personal theology.

self. Just as he is granted sympathy, he is allowed to argue with a freedom which Milton finds impossible to grant his conception of God as Abstract Reason. No wonder Blake is misled into his brilliant but partial intuition of the poem. Into Satan Milton pours all the power of his own passionate way of thinking; for God he reserves a purely theoretical process to arrive at the Absolute, and so the rational justification is foredoomed. Even the philosophical powers of Aquinas would not have enabled Milton to make completely logical what is supralogical, a matter for faith only; nor did the three hundred bishops at Nicaea have much better fortune. Milton himself recognizes this clearly in what amounts to an ironic comment on his own foolhardiness, when he says that the Fallen Angels in Hell

> reasoned high
> Of providence, foreknowledge, will and fate,
> Fixed fate, free will, foreknowledge absolute,
> *And found no end, in wandering mazes lost.*
>
> P.L., II, 558–61

Dante wisely avoids this problem by never letting God personally intrude into his poem. But Milton, unaware of his own mixed feelings toward reason, like Satan tries to usurp God's place, to reason for God. What Blake overlooks, however, is that this failure on the rational level neither completely invalidates nor exhausts Milton's characterization of the Deity, whose creativeness remains unimpaired. Milton is not so wise nor so honest in questioning and answering as that old Hebrew poet who wrote Job, but in the end he too finds sufficient answer in the magnitude and wonder of Creation.

If like Blake we allow ourselves to get caught in the maze of Milton's theological shortcomings and misguided ambition, we fail to appreciate another level on which the poem beautifully succeeds. For if the bold introduction of God is disastrous to Milton's justification by limited logic, it is essential to his marvelous portrayal of Creation, which, if any justification is needed, is enough.

Even the justifications and explanations which, when placed in God's mouth, inevitably put Him on the defensive and make Him open to fallacy, carry more conviction when Satan, as a character in a drama, utters them in his supreme moment of self-recognition:

> Ah wherefore! he deserved no such return
> From me, whom he created what I was
> In that bright eminence, and with his good
> Upbraided none; nor was his service hard.
> What could be less than to afford him praise,
> The easiest recompense, and pay him thanks,
> How due! yet all his good proved ill in me,
> And wrought but malice; lifted up so high
> I 'sdained subjection, and thought one step higher
> Would set me highest, and in a moment quit
> The debt immense of endless gratitude,
> So burdensome still paying, still to owe . . .
>
> P.L., IV, 42 ff.

The why, the wherefore, is purely rhetorical. Here is the heart of human frailty, that restless boredom of the ego which, while recognizing clearly the need to love, lacks the power to lose itself in love.

Believing passionately in the oneness of mind and body, Milton yet at the crucial point divorces too fatally passion and reason, granting all passion and much reason to Satan, while in those barren moments of needless self-justification stripping God of any warmth at all. Except always the warmth of Creation. Nothing shows more strikingly Milton's incapacity for that free and instinctive surrender to love found in Dante and Spenser than his approach to Christ, some aspects of whom he seems unconsciously, like Satan, to resent in his intolerance of any mediation between himself and God. Yet Christ is the key; Him, like Satan, we murder symbolically with our sin in the crucifixion, letting the dregs adverse to life blot out the light till the resurrection purges them downward again.

Milton's faltering reluctance toward Christ, however, is least apparent in *Paradise Lost*, where He appears as the Word, the Creator; for Milton's joy in creation is unalloyed. Though the last two books of the poem flag in inspiration, the triumph of God's plenitude is clear, and Milton's distrust of Romanism in abeyance, when Adam, echoing Raphael's beautiful first greeting to Eve, sings his Ave Maria:

> Virgin mother, hail,
> High in the love of heaven, yet from my loins
> Thou shalt proceed, and from thy womb the Son
> Of God most high . . .
>
> *P.L.*, XII, 379 ff.

The ambivalence of love-hate, life-death at the core of human life and the heart of Creation, personified in Milton's division between Satan and God, is no longer a question to be logically answered, but a mystery resolved. The faith is more mature (*Paradise Regained* seems to show it also less secure) but essentially the same as the Elder Brother's:

> But evil on itself shall back recoil,
> And mix no more with goodness, when at last
> Gathered like scum, and settled to itself
> It shall be in eternal restless change
> Self-fed, and self-consumed . . .
>
> *Comus*, 592 ff.

Unloosed hate is not merely yoked uneasily again with love but completely absorbed. Just as in the beginning by some strange alchemy, evil comes of good, so in the end this supreme manifestation of God's love brings forth good from evil—even, Milton firmly believes, greater good than was at first. Those who overstress the evangelical pessimism of *Paradise Lost* [19] should ponder:

> O goodness infinite, goodness immense!
> That all this good of evil shall produce,
> And evil turn to good; more wonderful
> Than that which by creation first brought forth
> Light out of darkness! full of doubt I stand,
> Whether I should repent me now of sin
> By me done and occasioned, or rejoice
> Much more, that much more good thereof shall spring,
> To God more glory, more good will to men
> From God, and *over wrath grace shall abound*.
>
> P.L., XII, 469–78

This from a blind old poet, whose long years of service to the Commonwealth of Saints had come to nought, whose political ideals had collapsed into the most dissolute of monarchies!

Not through reason, as he had planned, but through faith in God's grace, Creation comes full circle, ending as it begins, in Light.

[19] For example, Sir Herbert J. C. Grierson, *Milton and Wordsworth*, 97. Out of its seventeenth-century context Milton's austerity often seems merely grim to us.

III

Temptation

A<small>T THE LONG-EXPECTED</small>, foreknown climax of
Paradise Lost:

> She gave him of that fair enticing fruit
> With liberal hand: he scrupled not to eat
> *Against his better knowledge, not deceived,*
> *But fondly overcome with female charm.*
> Earth trembled from her entrails, as again
> In pangs, and nature gave a second groan . . .
> P.L., IX, 996 ff.

The temptation, so artfully prepared for, comes nonetheless with a sense of universal shock. Likewise, sharing
his anguish, we torment ourselves with Samson:

> what if all foretold
> Had been fulfilled but through mine own default,
> Whom have I to complain of but myself?
> Who this high gift of strength committed to me,
> In what part lodged, how easily bereft me,
> *Under the seal of silence could not keep,*
> *But weakly to a woman must reveal it,*
> *O'ercome with importunity and tears.*
> S.A., 44–51

This personal tragedy repeats in psychological detail the
original situation. Each act is compulsive, against all
knowledge, all true desire. And each taps a fundamental

stratum of deep emotional memories, the mystery of wrong choices made with eyes open yet blind.

On two other occasions Milton foils the tempter. With pagan-Christian eloquence the Lady heaps passionate scorn on Comus:

> And wouldst thou seek again to trap me here
> With liquorish baits fit to ensnare a brute?
> Were it a draught for Juno when she banquets,
> *I would not taste thy treasonous offer*; none
> But such as are good men can give good things,
> *And that which is not good, is not delicious*
> *To a well-governed and wise appetite.*
>
> *Comus*, 698–704

Many years later a far more ambitious and more disturbed poet has Christ put Satan behind him:

> To whom thus Jesus: 'Also it is written,
> "Tempt not the Lord thy God,"' he said and stood.
> But Satan smitten with amazement fell
> As when earth's son Antaeus (to compare
> Small things with greatest) in Irassa strove
> With Jove's Alcides, and oft foiled still rose,
> Receiving from his mother earth new strength,
> Fresh from his fall, and fiercer grapple joined,
> Throttled at length in the air, expired and fell;
> *So after many a foil the tempter proud,*
> *Renewing fresh assaults, amidst his pride*
> *Fell whence he stood to see his victor fall.*
>
> *P.R.*, IV, 560–71

Different as *Comus* and *Paradise Regained* are, nevertheless in portraying virtue absolute and unassailable in God's protection they are identical. This last climax dismisses temptation for good and all, thus fulfilling Milton's driving need; yet, so far as we know, he turns immediately to *Samson Agonistes*. Only then is all his passion spent.

The most striking thing about this repetitive design is Milton's single-minded preoccupation over a period of forty years in all his major and one of his two great minor poems with temptation. Even the elegiac waters of *Lycidas* are rippled as with a shark fin by the disturbing desire for fame and fear of choice. Two of these temptations are tragically successful, two triumphantly resisted. The successful temptations, more dramatically and psychologically developed, are profoundly moving revelations of universal experience. The two victories over temptation are relatively static elaborations of dogma in a personal epiphany. Confident though he sounds, Milton does not in his own terms convince us of virtue's triumph. And his final (though not necessarily conclusive) word is not victory—but defeat redeemed.

Examination of these four temptations carries us to the heart of Milton's mystery and spotlights an inner conflict which, as it waxes and wanes, largely determines the quality of his poetry. From the start a precarious relation between passion and reason is the core of the problem.

Comus and *Paradise Regained*, in the very course of demonstrating reason's triumph, show clearly that passion is always stronger in Milton than reason.[1] When he resents this supremacy and tries to throw off passion's yoke, he merely betrays more openly his own enthrallment; when he accepts it with little protest in *Paradise*

[1] Perhaps one difficulty in *Comus* is that the Lady's passion is deficient and misplaced, in *Paradise Regained* that the Passion of Christ is deliberately avoided for a mystic incident which Milton's age overextended almost into a first atonement.

Lost, or with bitter resignation in *Samson Agonistes,* he writes his greatest poetry. Without this agonizing ambivalence toward passion his poetry would have been altogether different and probably less memorable.

2.

Opinion of *Paradise Regained* will always be divided, and of late schism has developed in interpreting *Comus,* which, with all its central equivocations, is nonetheless a more successful poem than *Venus and Adonis* or the *Shepheardes Calender,* those comparable first ambitious flights of Shakespeare and Spenser. *Comus* almost succeeds in spite of itself. By sheer brilliance, by youthful exuberance of image and language, Milton almost convinces us that he has harmonized various modes and styles and reformulated myths while attempting a fresh variation on what was also Spenser's greatest concern— the reconciliation of pagan and Christian values. Much of the poem, except for the eloquent Puritan outbursts, works against the central dogmas so indirectly by rich imagery and veiled symbolism that we have a miraculous feeling of eating and having our cake, of reconciling Nature and Grace without quite knowing how, of admiring the beauty of chastity without paying the price of sterility. Basic contradictions, held temporarily in suspension by the magic of his verse, give an essentially static poem unpremeditated drama.

Yet, since Woodhouse's seminal study, the closer one examines *Comus* the more difficulties appear, the less certain final interpretation becomes. Steeped in Spenser and therefore inured to an eclectic, occasionally amorphous combination of allegory, symbol, myth, and psychological realism, Milton would probably be amazed by some of our fine-spun perplexities. Possibly we ask from a young poet more elaborate harmony of ideas than he himself intended. We should remember that he sees no incongruity in adapting two candid lines from Ovid's *Amores* in his own Latin elegies on the Bishop of Winchester and Spring.[2] Walking as delicately as possible, I am grateful to be concerned with the temptation theme only.

"Though chastity or temperance triumphs in the masque, the motif that is really dramatically interesting is the process of temptation," concludes D. C. Allen.[3] And in the development of this theme the Lady's virtue is predominantly chastity.

The mysterious wood, with its winding labyrinths, hidden springs, secret openings, is more than a part of the new Bridgewater domain. The wood has time-encrusted associations, as Dante knew when he began his

---

[2] Douglas Bush, *Mythology and the Renaissance Tradition*, 251.

[3] Allen, *The Harmonious Vision*, 39–40. Mr. Allen continues: "This is a theme dear to Milton's heart and one which he elaborated in all of his later works," incidentally corroborating the theme of this essay so remarkably that he might have been its genesis. Without entirely endorsing his view of *Comus*, I am in such complete agreement with his main belief that the poem fails to reconcile its opposites (without, however, regarding the failure as quite so serious) that I have revised several paragraphs in deference to his judgment. He overstresses the pre-texts (perhaps in reaction to those who brush them aside) and the importance of the time element.

I find the interpretation of *Comus* by Cleanth Brooks and John E. Hardy, *Poems of Mr. John Milton*, richly illuminating incidentally and a triumph of ingenuity; and find unexpected irony in so much rational moralizing from two anti-allegorists. I cannot agree that Milton's mind and imagination work in the metaphysical way Mr. Brooks and Mr. Hardy reconstruct. In this essential but delicate task of analysis Arnold Stein comes much closer to approximating Milton's imaginative processes.

Divine Comedy in *una selva oscura.* Like many of Spenser's forests or the wood in A *Midsummer Night's Dream* and *The Tempest,* Milton's is a world of magic, of mysteries and disguised symbols, both threatening and benevolent. Through it must pass the youthful trio, the Lady and her two brothers. Here Comus reigns, and more even than Satan of *Paradise Lost* he is a contradictory figure.

His contradiction matches the Lady's equivocation. No careful reader of the poem can feel that the Lady, any more than Shakespeare's Adonis, is merely a self-righteous prig; her scorn of Comus is too eloquent and moving to be lightly dismissed. And behind her protest, we know from other writings, is all the passionate restraint of Milton's own self-discipline till marriage.[4] In this doctrine of unassailable chastity what at once troubles us is sterility. Facing this difficulty in Belphoebe (ascetic chastity), Spenser solves it by creating her twin, Amoret (married chastity); but while Milton is following (at some distance, of course, and not exclusively) the Second and Third books of the *Faerie Queene* here, as he later writes *Paradise Regained* with eyes on Sir Guyon's Temptation by Mammon in the Second Book, he chooses to ignore until the very end this solution. Concerned with the three unmarried Bridgewater children, all he had to do was suggest less obscurely an exit from his false dilemma.

[4] For example, in *Doctrine and Discipline of Divorce:* "And lastly, it is not strange though many who have spent their youth in chastity are in some things not so quick-sighted . . ." The lines carry their own quality; but we can use such personal evidence to corroborate genuineness of emotion without in any sense converting the poem into verse biography.

Since he makes no attempt whatever to portray conflict in her mind, we know from the outset that the Lady
will remain virtuous. The whole poem is demonstration of dogmas passionately urged, not argued, since all
the argument is against them and only faith is for them.
A central dogma is formulated by the Elder Brother (the
masculine counterpart of the Lady, whereas the
Younger Brother is skeptical):

> So dear to heaven is saintly chastity,
> That when a soul is found sincerely so,
> *A thousand liveried angels lackey her,*
> *Driving far off each thing of sin and guilt . . .*
>   *Comus,* 452–55

by the Lady herself:

> O welcome pure-eyed faith, white-handed hope,
> *Thou hovering angel* girt with golden wings,
> *And thou unblemished form of chastity,*
> I see ye visibly, and now believe
> That he, the supreme good, to whom all things ill
> Are but as slavish officers of vengeance,
> *Would send a glistering guardian if need were*
> *To keep my life and honor unassailed.*
>   *Comus,* 212–19
> Thou hast nor ear, nor soul to apprehend
> The sublime notion, and *high mystery*
> That must be uttered to unfold the *sage*
> *And serious doctrine of virginity;*
>   *Comus,* 783–86

and by the Attendant Spirit at parting:

> Love virtue, *she alone is free,*
> She can teach ye how to climb
> Higher than the sphery chime;

Or if virtue feeble were,
Heaven itself would stoop to her.

Comus, 1018–22

We notice that chastity is a "sage and serious doctrine," [5] its "mystery" the only path to freedom; that in times of severest trial heavenly grace comes to the rescue, in various paraphrases of Psalm 91:11:

> For he shall give his angels charge over thee, to keep thee in all thy ways.

This same verse we shall find a pivot of *Paradise Regained.*[6]

Insofar as Comus represents license rather than liberty, the Lady's position is both strong and sympathetic. But Milton seems often in conflict with himself here. As if driven by some inner perversity, he grants Comus all those time-honored pleas for plenitude which Marlowe had used beautifully though half-cynically in *Hero and Leander,* Shakespeare with eloquent seriousness in his *Sonnets.* To understand fully how this confuses the issue we need only consider Milton's later poems.

We have already seen how in *Paradise Lost* he incorporates plenitude in all God's Creation as a specific injunction laid on sea, on land, on humankind. In

[5] This famous phrase, which Milton later applies to Spenser, suggests that he is thinking of the *Faerie Queene* here.
[6] Also, of course, of *Paradise Lost.* Satan particularly resents
> . . . flaming ministers to watch and tend
> Their earthly charge: Of these the vigilance
> I dread . . .

P.L., IX, 156 ff.

Woodhouse calls attention to Spenser's Platonic influence on the Brother's speech but neglects Milton's fondness for this key Biblical verse on grace.

Paradise Regained he reserves Christ's greatest scorn for the stoics. Yet by an extraordinary transposition, in *Comus* the Lady (at least by default) is the stoic, Comus plenitude:

> O foolishness of men! that lend their ears
> To those budge doctors of the Stoic fur,
> And fetch their precepts from the Cynic tub,
> Praising the lean and sallow abstinence.
> Wherefore did nature pour her bounties forth,
> With such a full and unwithdrawing hand,
> Covering the earth with odors, fruits, and flocks,
> Thronging the seas with spawn innumerable,
> But all to please, and sate the curious taste?
> . . . . . . *that no corner might*
> *Be vacant of her plenty . . .*

Then, in one of his finest passages Comus paints the wasted fertility of earth unused by nature's niggards:

> Who would be quite surcharged with her own weight,
> And strangled with her waste fertility;
> The earth cumbered, and the winged air darked with plumes.

Comus, 705 ff.

If Comus' argument represents sensuality, Milton himself adopts it when later he delights in pouring forth without stint God's bounties to please each sense, and creates in Adam the instrument perfectly adapted for their enjoyment.

Since the Lady's view of chastity (she may on another plane be called Continence, scarcely Temperance) is a dogma to be accepted without cavil, the rich persuasiveness not only of sensual luxury but of plenitude itself falls on ears of stone; she makes no attempt to distinguish between the two. And so her triumph is equivocal. While admiring her steadfastness, we cannot help suspecting that Comus' rich inducements simply do not appeal to her as they ought.

Further, the dogma of virginity, as Milton presents it, is impossibly limited, and with the failure of the dogma even the ritual struggle loses much of its meaning. Milton has kindled considerable expectation that in some way—through action or symbol—the Lady's "high mystery" will be indirectly revealed. Yet she seems merely repetitious and obstinately unyielding at the climax. When Comus' own argumentative eloquence suddenly falters in the only truly effective portrayal of Chastity's mysterious power—

> yet a cold shuddering dew
> Dips me all o'er, as when the wrath of Jove
> Speaks thunder, and the chains of Erebus
> To some of Saturn's crew—
>
> *Comus*, 801–804

the effect is marred because he attributes to "her words set off by some superior power" more virtue than those words convey. Unlike Allen, I find this sudden drying up of his eloquence a fine imaginative and dramatic stroke. But the stroke is premature, coming before the Lady has said anything to warrant it and before Comus has broached his final arguments. We are left suspecting that Milton did not want to risk Comus' full *counter*-argument mainly because he could not quite decide how to formulate the Lady's argument.

Whenever he is freed from his uncompromising elevation of the Elder Brother's faith and the Lady's impregnability, Milton elaborates with extraordinary zest the

other symbolism of the poem, and by a series of instinctive choices reveals his own divided allegiance. Whether
he was aware of it or not, his subject for the Lady's song
—Echo and Narcissus—is peculiarly appropriate. Chastity as the Lady portrays it and her Elder Brother exalts
it is strongly touched by narcissism, is a witholding of the
self akin to Belphoebe's cold aloofness, which troubled
Spenser. There is even a faint suggestion of latent
jealousy beneath the Elder Brother's passionate insist-
ence that the Lady remain untouched. Though the action at once proves the Elder Brother wrong, the skeptical Younger Brother right, Milton seems too preoccupied
to make effective use of this irony or even to fully recognize it.[7]

It is Comus, like Satan in *Paradise Lost*, who comes
nearest to liberating Milton's imagination by providing
a dramatic mouthpiece for arguing the other side with
good conscience. Comus in his "ominous wood," "ripe
and frolic of his full grown age," by his magic transforms the human countenance, "the express resemblance
of the gods," into brutish forms of wolf, bear, tiger, hog,
or goat. But this Circe-Acrasia element in his heritage
Milton for the most part treats with the tolerant indul-
gence of his favorite classical poets, creating none of
Spenser's deadly languor and sterility. The suggestion
that these grotesque figures in a comic anti-masque are

[7] Mr. Brooks and Mr. Hardy are at their best throughout this truly
dramatic part of *Comus*—the argument between the Elder and Younger
Brother and their first encounter with the Attendant Spirit. At this
point in the poem there is enough characterization for drama of this
kind and a genuine clash of temperaments. But none of these potentialities are realized beyond the scene where the two brothers rush in,
nor are they related to the concluding Sabrina incident.

the wages of self-indulgence and sin remains conventional and overshadowed.

If Comus' destructive qualities are only hinted at in the licentious orgies associated with Cotytto, "goddess of nocturnal sport," his positive qualities are brilliantly dominant. His power is derived not only from the god Bacchus, but on his mother's side from the sun, source of fertility; furthermore the sun influences mortals in Comus' behalf, since it is sun-induced thirst ("the drought of Phoebus") which makes them succumb to his magic cup—*for most do taste*. His father, Bacchus, is of course a favorite pagan symbol of generation—his liquors and grapes having a richer significance than mere intoxication. Comus himself is less demon than fertility god. In this struggle with Jove's deputies he does not win, but at least he remains in full control of his world; when Sabrina finally releases the Lady the Attendant Spirit urges swift flight, distrusting Comus' further spells.

Beneath his magic rites and midnight revels we sense an older allegiance, and, in the pulse of the verse, veiled mysteries of greater portent than the simple surface action and certainly more *poetically* realized than the Lady's "high mystery":

> We that are *of purer fire*
> Imitate the starry choir,
> Who in their nightly watchful spheres,
> Lead in swift round the months and years,
> The sounds, and seas with all their finny drove
> Now to the moon in wavering morris move,
> And on the tawny sands and shelves,
> Trip the pert fairies and the dapper elves;
> What hath night to do with sleep?
> Night hath better sweets to prove,

Venus now wakes, and wakens love.
Come let us our rites begin,
'Tis only daylight that makes sin . . .

Comus, 111 ff.

This is an echo of that familiar Elizabethan nostalgia for old "merry England" when an indulgent Church winked at belief in primitive survivals, even incorporated them into its own festivals. And Milton's symbolism of darkness and light, so clearly developed in his later poems, is here never completely clarified. He seems to be dealing with two sources of light and darkness which he fails to distinguish.

Milton does not consign the Lady to a cloister. After exposing her to the actuality of sex (and intemperance), he restores her temporarily to the bosom of her family. Comus' magic cup is dashed to the ground, but he keeps his *wand* and thus his phallic power. As a consequence the Attendant Spirit's plan goes awry and the Lady remains helplessly frozen in her chair.

This failure of the brothers, even with the help of two manifestations of heavenly grace (Attendant Spirit and magic haemony), can be variously explained (and I am not concerned with purely rational satisfaction), *if* Sabrina as a third and successful form of heavenly grace resolved the situation symbolically. But the Sabrina incident is the real crux. Interpretations of her intervention are so uniformly unsatisfactory that one suspects Milton's simple wish to increase opportunities for music and pageantry.[8] With Sabrina he returns to the typical

---

[8] Mr. Allen's suspicion that Milton originally may have planned a complete masque on Sabrina is plausible. At any rate the carpentry is not entirely successful here.

masque incident that delighted Inigo Jones. When she
is summoned to assist in freeing the Lady, her song-
induced emergence from the river inevitably suggests the
rich birth symbolism of Venus rising from the sea.
Though she proclaims that her office is "to help ensnared
chastity," few passages in the poem are more unadulter-
atedly pagan in feeling, and many of her companions,
like old Proteus and the sirens, accord far better with
Circe and Comus.

Finally, in his curiously ambiguous parting speech the
Attendant Spirit does not withdraw into ascetic contem-
plation but, though he calls it Hesperides, to Spenser's
Garden of Adonis, nurturing place of Amoret, where
marriage becomes finally explicit:

> Where young Adonis oft reposes,
> Waxing well of his deep wound
> In slumber soft, and on the ground
> Sadly sits the Assyrian queen;
> But far above in spangled sheen
> Celestial Cupid her famed son advanced,
> Holds his dear Psyche sweet entranced
> After her wandering labors long,
> Till free consent the gods among
> Make her his eternal bride . . .

Comus, 998–1007

With this suggestion Milton leaves us, after demonstrating in beautiful eclectic poetry the powerful pull of two
forces which he neither succeeds in reconciling nor even
in quite balancing harmoniously. Tension in *Comus*
comes less from the ritualistic clash of Nature and Grace
or sensuality and chastity than from this ambivalence
pervading imagery and symbolism.

3.

To turn from *Comus*, in which Milton by imagination
and instinct almost overcomes a central rigidity, to
Paradise Regained, which after some forty years resumes
this same formula in a new guise, is illuminating. The
later poem shifts emphasis from the body's to the mind's
passion; but the two are never completely separate in
Milton. Several passages even in *Comus* indicate that
he is preoccupied with purity of mind as well as body,
with the problem of letting the mind range freely and
independently without contamination. Comus' spell, *un-
moulding reason's image charactered in the face*, replaces
it with a brute's. By his magic passion he freezes helplessly the Lady's body, so that she is like Daphne "root-
bound," but

> Fool do not boast
> *Thou canst not touch the freedom of my mind . . .*
> Comus, 662 ff.

Milton in *Paradise Lost* does not leave Christ's offer
through love to sacrifice himself for man a mere promise;
in Adam's dream he shows its triumphant fulfillment:

> Not by destroying Satan, but his works
> In thee and in thy seed: nor can this be,
> But by fulfilling that which thou didst want,
> *Obedience to the law of God, imposed*
> *On penalty of death, and suffering death,*
> *The penalty of thy transgression due,*
> And due to theirs which out of thine will grow:
> So only can high justice rest appaid.
> *The law of God exact he shall fulfill*
> *Both by obedience and by love, though love*

Alone fulfill the law . . . . . .
For this he shall live hated, be blasphemed,
Seized on by force, judged, and to death condemned
A shameful and accursed, nailed to the cross
By his own nation, slain for bringing life;
But to the cross he nails thy enemies,
The law that is against thee, and the sins
Of all mankind, with him there crucified,
Never to hurt them more who rightly trust
In this his satisfaction; so he dies,
But soon revives, death over him no power
Shall long usurp; ere the third dawning light
Return, the stars of morn shall see him rise
Out of his grave, fresh as the dawning light,
Thy ransom paid . . .

                                        P.L., XII, 394 ff.

This is the Scriptural way by which man regains Paradise.

After reading these lines we are baffled by Thomas Ellwood's fatuous suggestion that *Paradise Lost* leaves man's redemption unexplained. Why should Milton feel further need to treat this subject, except perhaps in an elaboration of Christ's life, crucifixion, resurrection from the dead? He thought long and often about Christ, as we learn from the Trinity Manuscript as well as his published works. We remember that forty years earlier he calls Christ

> Most perfect hero, *tried in heaviest plight*
> *Of labors huge and hard, too hard for human wight.*
> . . . .
> These latest scenes confine my roving verse,
> To this horizon is my Phoebus bound,
> His godlike acts; *and his temptations fierce,*
> *And former sufferings otherwhere are found . . .*

This poem, *The Passion*, he gave over, "finding to be above the years he had" in 1630.

When he returns to Christ after *Paradise Lost* he ignores the Passion, because he has become obsessed with temptation. Also, we must recognize that Milton was strongly affected by the still vital tradition (coming down through the Middle Ages, modified by Renaissance and Reformation) that Christ submitted to temptation in order to restore to man the capacity of resistance which Adam had lost. During his last fruitful years, while winding up *Paradise Lost*, Milton must have been simultaneously planning both *Paradise Regained* and *Samson Agonistes*, neither of them a product of sudden inspiration. These three poems suggest in their contradictions that, in spite of vehement statements, he never fully resolves his central conflict, that two dramatizations of defeat in Adam and Samson make it imperative at all cost that he show man in better light.

It is ironic that the poet who writes so eloquently of virtue in action—"I cannot praise a fugitive and cloistered virtue, unexercised and unbreathed"—should find his two examples of virtue's triumph in a young inexperienced girl and untried Christ before his active career begins, though his second choice seemed more natural to the seventeenth century. Not so deeply involved personally in *Comus*, he almost manages to make a virtue of ambiguity. But he cannot extricate himself and his unresolved conflicts in *Paradise Regained*, which for all the surface serenity of Christ is poetically most noteworthy for its passages of deep hostility, recalling the "dread voice" which disturbs *Lycidas* and the unrestrained vituperation of his polemical tracts. In spite of

its fine "majestic unaffected style," its mature crafts-
manship and polish, *Paradise Regained* is a throwback
to Milton's turbulent years and the most clouded work
he ever produced in verse. Conceived in an elaborate
tradition now outmoded,[9] the poem compromises with
and departs from that tradition in obscure, sometimes
inexplicable fashion.

It seems more a postscript to *Paradise Lost* than a
sequel; a long poetic footnote in which Milton, while
balancing temptations, pours out his personal dissatisfaction with the Genesis story of Original Sin, which he
seemed to accept earlier. Christ gives Satan the answers
which Adam and Eve *should* have given. The occasional
vehemence is possibly reaction from the self-imposed
restraint of *Paradise Lost*, in which Milton manages to
keep even his heresies unobtrusive. In his heart of
hearts he can not regard Adam's temptation as quite
fair. It is not enough for Christ to redeem; he must
avenge Adam.[10] As Mr. Willey diagnoses the problem:

> But this limited freedom of choice, and its arbitrary
> connection with an inexplicable taboo, did not consti-
> tute the full 'liberty' of Milton's ripest thought. A man
> must *know good and evil* much more intimately than
> prelapsarian Adam could before he can submit with his
> whole being to the control of that divine law in whose
> service is perfect freedom . . . Milton was a Prome-
> thean, a Renaissance humanist, in the toils of a myth
> of quite contrary import, a myth which yearned, as no

[9] Miss Elizabeth Pope in *Paradise Regained: The Tradition and the
Poem* demonstrates that a general acquaintance with the tradition is
essential to understanding the poem.

[10] See *P.R.*, IV, 606–607: "now thou hast avenged/Supplanted
Adam."

Milton could, for the blank innocence and effortlessness of a golden age.[11]

Though we no longer consider Milton exclusively a Renaissance Promethean, this is acute, so far as it goes. But does not the Lady of *Comus* in her absolute and unassailable virtue show yearning for "innocence and effortlessness" impervious by its very nature to evil? Milton can no more dispense entirely with the myth of a golden world where Reason automatically banishes evil than he can give up his personal conception of freedom. He tries to reformulate the myth, returning to a theme of his boyhood in the *Nativity Ode:* with Christ's coming all pagan oracles cease (*P.R.*, I, 455–65). No one knew better the persistence of these "pagan oracles" in Restoration England; yet Milton's desire is so intense that, like St. Paul (even while warning against the expectation), he peremptorily longs for the Second Coming immediately. By his victory over temptation, Christ not only avenges "supplanted Adam" and regains lost Paradise, frustrating the "conquest fraudulent"; but also Satan

> . . . never more henceforth will dare set foot
> In Paradise to tempt; his snares are broke:
> For though that seat of earthly bliss be failed,
> A fairer Paradise *is founded now*
> For Adam and his chosen sons . . .
>
> . . . .
> Where *they shall dwell secure,* when time shall be
> *Of tempter and temptation without fear* . . .
> > > > *P.R.*, IV, 610 ff.

What is this but fear of temptation and yearning for

[11] Basil Willey, *The Seventeenth Century Background,* 255.

the "innocence and effortlessness of a golden age" not of striving but security?

Miss Pope has shown that we must guard against shifts of scriptural emphasis since the seventeenth century. Still, it is a severe limitation if the poem makes sense *only* in terms of an outmoded convention. While ostensibly repeating temptations in order to redeem what has gone before and bring the past into intelligible relation with present and future, Milton's instinctive drive often seems to *cancel* the original fatal temptation and *undo* the past. There are occasional moments of powerful wish fulfillment. Perhaps this will be clearer if we examine briefly the scriptural incident and what Milton makes of it, for he certainly interpreted the actual text for himself before consulting traditional commentaries. What he leaves out is as significant as what he adds.

4.

The scriptural story demonstrates the power and truth of the Bible, for in this simple narrative Christ makes no attempt to outreason Satan, whom he defeats merely by quoting three verses from Deuteronomy, God's Word to Moses. To the first temptation that he turn stones into bread to assuage his hunger, Christ replies with the key phrase:

> And he humbled thee, and suffered thee to hunger, and fed thee with manna, which thou knewest not, neither did thy fathers know, that he might make thee know that *man doth not live by bread only, but by every word that proceedeth out of the mouth of the Lord* doth man live. (Deuteronomy 8:3)

To Satan's offer of worldly power and riches if Christ only will worship him, Christ answers:

> *Thou shalt fear the Lord thy God, and serve him,* and shalt swear by his name. (Deuteronomy 6:13)

Finally, Christ replies to Satan's suggestion that he prove his divinity by dashing himself from the Temple to be spectacularly rescued in midair:

> *Ye shall not tempt the Lord your God* as ye tempted him in Massah. (Deuteronomy 6:16)

St. Luke concludes his version, which Milton chooses in preference to St. Matthew's:

> And when the devil had ended all the temptations, he departed from him *for a season.* (Luke 4:13)

Not for good, as Milton has it, "for a season" only. This initial formal temptation illuminates the whole subsequent Gospel account of Christ's life. Not only does he later perform those very miracles suggested by Satan—miracles of producing food, turning water into wine, raising people from the dead; he is also constantly under pressure to turn these miracles to quick wordly advantage and his own personal ends. Again and again he has to retire from the press of people to meditate and pray and strengthen his spirit. The Pharisees, like Satan, constantly seek to entrap him in Scripture. Continuing St. Luke, we come to the Agony in Gethsemane (22:40–46):

> And when he was at the place, he said unto them, *"Pray that ye enter not into temptation."* And he was withdrawn from them about a stone's cast, and kneeled down, and prayed, saying, "Father, if thou be willing,

remove this cup from me: nevertheless, not my will, but thine, be done." *And there appeared an angel unto him from heaven, strengthening him.* And being in an agony he prayed more earnestly: and *his sweat was as it were great drops of blood falling down to the ground.* . . . "Why sleep ye? rise and pray, *lest ye enter into temptation.*"

Milton, who knows his Bible by heart and has genius for Biblical mosaic, deliberately ignores this profound development of Christ's persistent temptations, even though the Trinity Manuscript shows that at one time he planned a poem on the Agony in the Garden. Of course the most obvious answer is that the seventeenth century elaborated the Temptation of Christ as an incident complete in itself, that Milton was conditioned by his age. But the significant point is that none of Milton's several independent departures from the tradition suggest the power of persistent temptation; all hammer home to us Christ's complete unsusceptibility.

A twentieth-century reader, after finishing *Paradise Regained,* reasonably asks, "What does Christ do here that Job has not already done, and not by pure reason?" Milton overlooks what he has himself so beautifully portrayed in *Paradise Lost*—that it is no longer Satan alone whom we must overcome, but Sin and Death, since Adam is inherent in us from birth. Instead of the great poem of redemption which its title and *Paradise Lost* seem to promise, our generation finds a lyrical epic which remains the most private and inaccessible of all his works, even after we learn its background and grasp the double focus (Christ and Milton).

One modern solution is to minimize Christian significance. Milton of course is perfectly free to write a Unitarian or Socinian rather than Christian poem, and this view Miss Mahood, following Mr. Willey's suggestion, tacitly accepts when she interprets *Paradise Regained* as an inner debate of a great humanist on true glory, and thus makes persuasive partial sense of it. To clarify her view, however, she arbitrarily dismisses the first and third temptations:

> Milton . . . is not greatly concerned with the first and third assays by which Satan tries to entice the Saviour into a miraculous display of His divine powers. *They fall outside the scope of his intention to show Christ as the perfect man.* Accordingly, in Milton's poem, the first temptation merely serves the purpose of bringing the protagonists together in the sharp enmity that follows their mutual recognition, and the third temptation, culminating in Satan's fall, is reduced to the outward symbol of the victory Christ has already won in His abnegation of wordly power. *Since Milton is dealing with a humanist problem he concentrates all the dramatic interest of the work on the one temptation out of the three which was within the experience of the human mind at its heroic best.*[12]

If this be true, surely Milton had the dramatic instinct simply to choose St. Matthew's version, which places this humanistic victory over worldly power last, and which also happened to be the traditional favorite. But the text shows why he chooses St. Luke's order, and also why he chooses Christ rather than Job or Socrates or some great humanist as his "perfect man." Though Miss Mahood considers only the second temptation "within the experience of the human mind at its heroic best,"

[12] M. M. Mahood, *Poetry and Humanism,* 233–34. Italics mine.

Milton makes explicitly clear that *any* good and wise man could have overcome the *first two* temptations, after which Satan remarks:

> And opportunity I here have had
> To try thee, sift thee, and confess have found thee
> Proof against all temptations as a rock
> Of adamant, and as a center, *firm*
> *To the utmost of mere man both wise and good,*
> *Not more;* for honors, riches, kingdoms, glory
> Have been before contemned, and may again:
> Therefore *to know what more thou art than man*
> *Worth naming Son of God by voice from heaven,*
> Another method I must now begin.
>
> P.R., IV, 531–40

Testing the *divinity* not the humanity of Christ is Satan's motive.

What Miss Mahood completely overlooks is that, while Milton ignores the rich implications of Christ's subsequent career, he draws exhaustively on St. Luke's opening chapters—the *Annunciation*, the *Magnificat*, the *Nunc Dimittis* of Simeon, Christ's visit to the Temple at twelve. Most significant of all, he stresses, not once but several times, St. John's baptism of Christ, when in that most striking manifestation of the Trinity in all Scripture, God Himself cries out as the Dove appears: "Thou art my beloved Son; in thee I am well pleased." No one can deny the Socinian touches, which are especially marked in the interludes where Christ is a mask for the poet himself; nonetheless Milton emphasizes remarkably this manifestation of the Trinity and Mary's exalted meditation at the opening of the Second Book on the mystery of her Son:

> but now
> Full grown to man, acknowledged, as I hear,
> By John the Baptist, and in public shown,
> Son owned from heaven by his father's voice;
> I looked for some great change; to honor? no,
> But trouble, as old Simeon plain foretold,
> That to the fall and rising he should be
> Of many in Israel, and to a sign
> Spoken against, that through my very soul
> A sword shall pierce . . .
>
> *P.R.*, II, 82 ff.

Having many years earlier based *Comus* partly on Psalm 91:11, Milton could hardly fail to be struck by the fact that it is precisely this verse, this article of faith, that Satan in the third temptation demands that Christ prove:

> Cast thyself down; safely if Son of God:
> For it is written: "He will give command
> Concerning thee to his angels, in their hands
> They shall uplift thee, lest at any time
> Thou chance to dash thy foot against a stone."
>
> *P.R.*, IV, 555–59

In the moment of Christ's Agony in the Garden, God fulfills His Word—*And there appeared an angel unto him from heaven, strengthening him.* But Satan is here tempting Christ to premature, scientific proof of God's promise, thus insinuating doubt. This is the only temptation which Milton does not elaborate or comment upon; his Christ answers in the words of St. Luke, and Satan falls. Consequently, this third temptation remains somewhat enigmatic[13] in the confusing crosscurrents of

---

[13] "This is certainly not a conventional temptation of the tower. It is not even a temptation in the ordinary sense at all."—Pope, *Paradise Regained: The Tradition and the Poem*, 94.

Paradise Regained; yet it cannot reasonably be dismissed or reduced to humanistic symbolism.

Up to this point Christ is clearly any wise and good man armed with God's Revealed Truth and, to Milton more potent even, God-given knowledge of what is right, which he felt Adam insufficiently possessed. In such a situation Milton is convinced that reason chooses the right as irresistibly as iron turns to a magnet. Satan in *Paradise Regained* is impotent from the start and knows it; and Christ himself at times seems almost bored by this ritualistic "trial" (though of course the ritual with its established pattern had deeper appeal to the seventeenth century):

> Why dost thou then suggest to me distrust,
> Knowing who I am, as I know who thou art?
>
> P.R., I, 355–56

By the mere process of discarding much Roman, Anglican, and Calvinist doctrine, Milton is forced back on his own interpretation of Scripture as his ultimate personal dogma, to surrender which would be annihilation of all belief. This may be one reason why he refuses to elaborate the final temptation. Under the surface of the suggestion that Christ dash himself from the Temple one feels an uneasy presence, which disturbs Christian commentators, in Samson's dying in order to destroy the Philistines (and which Miss Pope reminds us was even suggested by two contemporary interpretations of the Third Temptation)—suicide. In *Paradise Regained* Milton seems narrowly to escape the suicide of his own faith by clinging to his personal dogma. Tertullian puts his finger on the danger when he remarks:

"Familiarity with the Scripture has its roots in the ruminating spirit. The thirst for knowledge takes the place of belief; the thirst for fame takes the place of spiritual welfare. To know nothing contrary to the rules of faith is to know everything!" [14]

This sheds more light on *Paradise Regained* than the humanistic explanation. For Milton's dogmatic conception of Reason, taken literally, would nullify the whole poem if he were not so unconsciously on the defensive, so anxious to be Renaissance humanist and staunch Christian together, if he did not have a compulsive need to defend what he protests needs no defense.

5.

To unravel this enigma completely is impossible even for those who have painstakingly searched the tradition. But it may help to examine closely the three interludes which Milton inserts after he has extended Scripture even farther than the Biblical commentators. It is not surprising to find that if we could simply omit these overlapping interludes, which make *Paradise Regained* Milton's most repetitious and discursive poem, we should come close to eliminating the difficulties. Yet to eliminate them would take away the best poetry and most of the drama. It is of course in the interludes that Christ is a thin disguise for Milton, resisting not so much His own but Milton's particular perils.[15]

The first temptation, according to Miss Mahood,

[14] Quoted by Theodor Reik, *Dogma and Compulsion,* 114.
[15] Long ago Legouis remarked, and Tillyard subsequently demonstrated, that Milton, not King, is the real subject of *Lycidas.* Milton *intrudes* in *Paradise Regained;* he does not dominate this poem as he does *Lycidas.*

"merely serves the purpose of bringing the protagonists together in the sharp enmity that follows their mutual recognition." She is right only if we limit ourselves to the formal treatment. The original appeal to hunger in the First Book is brief, only slightly developed by the addition from Old Testament stories of similar hunger felt by Moses and Elijah. Indeed, Christ crushes him with such ease that Satan is stung to long self-defense, boasting (unfortunately from his point of view, but in this poem Milton is not consistently interested in characterization) that God gave Job into His hands to tempt. This enables Christ to dismiss literal food and expatiate on the difference between falsehood and truth; for "lying," says Christ, "is thy sustenance, thy food." So far, then, the temptation of food is little more than excuse for digression.[16]

Night falls. Milton takes advantage of the pause to dramatize more exposition, in the opening of the Second Book portraying the dismay of the disciples and the worried musings of Mary. Then abruptly we shift to Satan's consultation with his Fallen Angels, during which he no longer bothers to hide his scorn of their advice:

> Therefore with manlier objects we must try
> His constancy, with such as have more show
> Of worth, of honor, glory, and popular praise.
> P.R., II, 225–27

[16] Miss Pope reveals a cogent reason for this vacillation by Protestant theologians in interpreting temptation by bread. And she advances an interesting theory that the banqueting scene is Milton's way of combining Protestant and Catholic interpretations in his determination to make this a genuine temptation of the flesh. *Paradise Regained: The Tradition and the Poem*, 70 ff. Spenser of course stressed the importance of food in Sir Guyon's case.

But when Satan next confronts Christ, to our surprise he resumes the temptation to hunger. With Christ his hero, Milton is forced to omit sensual temptation through sex, which he uses in his other three poems on this theme. Yet gluttony is sensual, sex itself a kind of hunger; and so in *Paradise Regained* food is made to bear the whole burden of the temptation of the flesh. Since we have already seen how fond Milton is in all his poetry of imagery and symbolism of eating, it is not surprising to find in this interlude on food that the appeal to stark hunger is more varied and psychologically penetrating than at first appears.

During the night Christ has "dreamed, as appetite is wont to dream," of Elijah miraculously fed—a double miracle, since the ravenous ravens violate their own nature in bringing his food untouched. Now Satan abandons the suggestion that Christ by a miracle turn stones into bread. Instead he summons a miraculous banquet of his own, with accompaniment of soft music, sweet odors, and (showing that he has not after all been unimpressed by Belial's suggestion) nymphs more beautiful than any known to fable or song. For sheer poetic beauty nothing else in the poem surpasses this banquet; its direct appeal is sensuality, uncomplicated by risk of selfish miracle on Christ's part. But Christ, though he *now* has strong appetite for food, as he did not during the previous forty days' fasting (*P.R.*, 245–49), is still

> fed with better thoughts that feed
> Me hungering more to do my father's will.

He scornfully rejects this feast likewise, but evidently it lingers in his mind, for at the height of the second temptation in the Fourth Book, he himself mentions food among the luxuries of empire,[17] only to reject it a third time:

> Nor doth this grandeur and majestic show
> Of luxury, though called magnificence,
> More than of arms before, allure mine eye,
> Much less my mind; *though thou shouldest add to tell*
> *Their sumptuous gluttonies, and gorgeous feasts*
> *On citron tables or Atlantic stone;*
> (For I have also heard, perhaps have read)
> Their wines of Setia, Cales, and Falerne,
> Chios and Crete, and how they quaff in gold,
> Crystal and myrrhine cups embossed with gems
> And studs of pearl . . .
>
> P.R., IV, 110 ff.

Furthermore, Milton keeps reminding us of Christ's hunger, which is his unifying symbol, modulated from food to truth to glory. The whole of the Second Book and the opening of the Third are actually two interlocked interludes on hunger of the flesh, hunger for truth, hunger for glory; for it is not till halfway through the Third that Milton picks up the setting of the second temptation:

> With that (such power was given him then) he took
> The Son of God up to a mountain high . . .
>
> P.R., III, 251–52

Thus Milton's development of the first temptation is abrupt dismissal for a digression on truth, then a second more poetically brilliant and symbolically rich appeal to

---

[17] This reappearance may be partly traditional, since Miss Pope informs us that banqueting was usually associated with the temptation of the kingdoms.

sensuality, strong enough to linger in Christ's mind (or Milton's) long after it has been refused. In between these two trials by food, however, comes the first seriously disturbing passage in the poem, not only because it is overvehement, but also because it is irrelevant to Christ. It is of course relevant to Milton, the actual hero of these interludes, or to Milton replaying Adam's role.

When Satan asks advice of his followers, Belial responds with all the eloquence of Milton's own passionate nature:

> Set women in his eye and in his walk,
> Among daughters of men the fairest found;
> Many are in each region passing fair
> As the noon sky; more like to goddesses
> Than mortal creatures, graceful and discreet,
> Expert in amorous arts, enchanting tongues
> Persuasive, virgin majesty with mild
> And sweet allayed, yet terrible to approach,
> Skilled to retire, and in retiring draw
> Hearts after them tangled in amorous nets.
> Such object hath the power to soften and tame
> Severest temper, smooth the ruggedest brow,
> Enerve, and with voluptuous hope dissolve,
> Draw out with credulous desire, and *lead*
> *At will the manliest, resolutest breast,*
> *As the magnetic hardest iron draws* . . .
>
> P.R., II, 153 ff.

Satan is quick to answer with a long impassioned speech from Milton's alter ego:

> what woman will you find,
> Though of this age the wonder and the fame,
> On whom his leisure will vouchsafe an eye
> Of fond desire? or should she confident,
> As sitting queen adored on beauty's throne,
> Descend with all her winning charms begirt

To enamor, as the zone of Venus once
Wrought that effect on Jove, so fables tell;
How would one look from his majestic brow
Seated as on the top of virtue's hill,
Discountenance her despised, and put to rout
All her array; her female pride deject,
Or turn to reverent awe? *for beauty stands*
In the admiration only of weak minds
Led captive; cease to admire, and all her plumes
Fall flat and shrink into a trivial toy . . .

P.R., II, 208 ff.

Satan steps out of character. The scornful tone here—
seated as on the top of virtue's hill—inevitably and a
little uncomfortably recalls the Lady in *Comus.* But it is
the sweeping, indiscriminate contempt for beauty and
woman that antagonizes us.

Since he goes on to symbolize effectively Christ's
weakness of the flesh by hunger for food, why should
Milton wilfully intrude this turbulent passage flatly
denying the heroic stature of his own Adam and Samson? Knowing that Christ in Holy Scripture is for some
mysterious reason never exposed to this particular temptation, we cannot help resisting Milton's exploitation for
a dubious victory. Nor is his case improved by associat-
ing with Christ, as two brother heroes bent on higher,
manlier aims than pursuit of beauty, Alexander of Mace-
don and Scipio Africanus!

This denial of beauty, dragged in to the embarrass-
ment of the poem, is savage and inept. Yet Milton is
directing the anguished command, "Cease to admire,"
not so much to Adam and Samson and us, as to himself.
Then, scarcely a hundred lines later he writes from the
other side of his nature:

distant more
Under the trees now tripped, now solemn stood
Nymphs of Diana's train, and naiades
With fruits and flowers from Amalthea's horn,
And ladies of the Hesperides, that seemed
Fairer than feigned of old or fabled since . . .

P.R., II, 353–58

All three passages—Belial's fearful, irresistible tribute, the hostility to beauty, and this astonishingly serene evocation—immediately kindle the ascetic style of *Paradise Regained* to pulsing life, revealing underneath the surface a violent crosscurrent of ambivalent emotions, which while producing his finest poetry and drama temporarily wreck his poem.

Equally bewildering, Milton anticipates the temptation to glory in the interlude preceding its formal statement, so that the actual temptation is drained of any impact it might have had. And to explain this by supposing that he must defend his own interpretation against traditional theology does not help the poem. After Christ resists the suggestion that he produce his own miracle food or partake of Satan's miraculous banquet, Satan, still using the underlying symbolism of hunger, appeals to "thirst for glory." The lure of this prospect leaves Christ calm but contemptuous:

Thou neither dost persuade me to seek wealth
For empire's sake, nor empire to affect
For glory's sake by all thy argument.
For what is glory but the blaze of fame,
The people's praise, if always praise unmixed?
And what the people but a herd confused,
A miscellaneous rabble, who extol
Things vulgar, and well weighed, scarce worth the
   praise.

They praise and they admire they know not what;

. . . .

Of whom to be dispraised were no small praise?
His lot who dares be singularly good.

P.R., III, 44 ff.

This reworking of a theme from *Lycidas* might be appropriate to a Renaissance philosopher-prince; it is grating and out of key here. Aristocratic contempt for the mob, though we may feel some agreement ourselves (if based on wisdom, surely it is worldly not heavenly wisdom), ill suits the Saviour of Mankind who chose to live and work as a carpenter and preach among the ignorant and poor, whose scorn was reserved for money-changers and abusers of privilege. Even when we realize that this is really Milton talking, we suspect his candor, knowing how long he hungered and thirsted for public glory as writer and statesman.

Still, this prepares for the finest conception of true glory to be found in the poem, when Christ in a speech that might come from *Paradise Lost* rebukes Satan for saying that God Himself insatiably demands glory from all:

And reason; since his word all things produced,
Though chiefly *not for glory as prime end,*
But to show forth his goodness, and impart
His good communicable to every soul
Freely; of whom what could he less expect
Than glory and benediction, that is thanks,
The slightest, easiest, readiest recompense

. . . .

But why should man seek glory? who of his own
Hath nothing, and to whom nothing belongs
But condemnation, ignominy, and shame?
Who for so many benefits received

Turned recreant to God, ingrate and false,
And so of all true good himself despoiled,
Yet, sacrilegious, to himself would take
That which to God alone of right belongs;
Yet so much bounty is in God, such grace,
That who advance his glory, not their own,
Them he himself to glory will advance.

                                   P.R., III, 122 ff.

This strikes Satan dumb. It is a truth which he himself has recognized almost in these terms in his famous soliloquy at the opening of the Fourth Book of *Paradise Lost*.[18] Never in command of the situation as he is with Eve, facing a far more formidable antagonist than Adam, Satan at this point has the tables completely turned, his own reason against himself. Already he has tempted Christ with riches, worldly power, and glory. Now senselessly he tries military power, and, just when we consider this phase of the temptation over, we discover that it is only formally beginning!

Satan, through a train of reasoning cogent only to Milton and students of the tradition,[19] chooses this moment to appear in his true colors to Christ, who has pierced his disguise at their first encounter (*P.R.*, I, 356), and to offer Christ, who has already dismissed these bribes, the identical bribes all over again, provided

[18] Quoted on p. 84.
[19] Miss Pope reminds us that tradition provides a thread here: "Thus, the devil first offers Christ great riches—to enable him to become a king; then popular acclaim—to result from his assumption of the Jewish throne; then armed might—to be won by his taking command of Parthia; then earthly luxury and magnificence—to be achieved by his making himself emperor of Rome. . . ."—*Paradise Regained: The Tradition and the Poem*, 66. Outmoded rituals survive in literature only when the ritual, no longer entirely understood, still meets some emotional or psychological need.

Christ pay the exorbitant price of worshipping Satan instead of God! No amount of elucidation can reconcile the present-day reader to what appears a perverse flouting of credibility and drama. If this is the tradition, then Milton as artist should have recognized its dramatic shortcomings. He was surely a poet first, a theologian second, and had already demonstrated in *Paradise Lost* genius for reducing elaborate tradition to poetic and dramatic simplicity.

Heretofore Satan has held our interest in his desperately shifting moods; suddenly he ceases to make any sense at all as the great Adversary, nor has Milton revealed in Christ any traits which suggest susceptibility to these new gambits. Overanxious to convince himself and us of his contempt for the tempter, Milton deprives Satan of mind and the temptation of meaning.[20]

Just as the poem momentarily collapses under us, Milton introduces his final interlude. Satan gets a second wind, dismisses worldly glory for intellectual renown,[21] and in the process dismisses Christ for Milton himself:

> Be famous then
> By wisdom; as thy empire must extend,
> So let extend thy mind o'er all the world,
> In knowledge, all things in it comprehend,
> All knowledge is not couched in Moses' law,
> The Pentateuch or what the prophets wrote,
> The Gentiles also know, and write, and teach
> To admiration, led by nature's light . . .
>   *P.R.*, IV, 221 ff.

---

[20] The most persuasive and subtle case for Satan's characterization is that of D. C. Allen (*The Harmonious Vision*, 110 ff.), but I am not quite persuaded.

[21] This, as Miss Pope reminds us, is entirely Milton's addition.

That Milton should take this opportunity to exalt the glory of the Bible and Hebrew literature none can wonder; yet as he proceeds to damn classic literature and wisdom, to which so many years of his own life have been dedicated, from which his own poetry draws such rich nourishment, we again find bitterness out of all proportion to the ostensible occasion:

> Remove their swelling epithets thick laid
> *As varnish on a harlot's cheek*, the rest,
> Thin sown with aught of profit or delight,
> Will far be found unworthy to compare
> With Sion's songs . . .
>
> P.R., IV, 343 ff.

This repudiates not only the florid Ovid but the style in which he himself has just written *Paradise Lost* and a few of the best passages of this very poem. And this rationalization[22] comes from the powerful and independent intellect that conceived *Areopagitica*.

We sense deep disillusion in the sweeping condemnation:

> Who therefore seeks in these
> True wisdom, finds her not, or by delusion
> Far worse, her false resemblance only meets,
> An empty cloud.

True wisdom is in man's reason or inner light:

> However many books
> Wise men have said are wearisome; who reads
> Incessantly, and to his reading brings not
> *A spirit and judgment equal or superior,*

---

[22] Milton's position seems to be that since Holy Scripture is Divinely —not just divinely—inspired it must be superior, regardless of the human instrument, in every respect, including literary grace.

(*And what he brings, what needs he elsewhere seek*)
Uncertain and unsettled still remains,
Deep versed in books and shallow in himself,
Crude or intoxicate, collecting toys,
And trifles for choice matters, worth a sponge;
As children gathering pebbles on the shore.

                                        P.R., IV, 318–30

Ostensibly this is an attack on fruitless study. But Milton does not stop with the wise recognition that books are meaningless, confusing, more harmful than good without innate judgment; he retreats to the citadel of his own mind in the parenthesis which negates learning like an Alexandrian bonfire—*And what he brings, what needs he elsewhere seek.* Just as he turned in suicidal fury on beauty, which long inspired and tormented him, he now turns and rips to shreds the passion of fifty years. Perish all writing save the Bible. Is not Milton here close to Tertulian's mind: "To know nothing contrary to the rules of faith is to know everything?"

The tired despair of this revulsion keeps us from resenting its savagery, all the more terrible in that *Paradise Regained* is not a brief lyric outburst but a sustained poem requiring time and meditation to compose. Milton, while leaving us instructed if not convinced about the temptations of Christ, reveals clearly the sources of his own temptation even to the verge of defeat. By refusing to accept defeat he overcomes it to what extent no man can say, at least sufficiently to climax his poem with affirmation: "Tempt not the Lord thy God."

Then, with no sense of incongruity, the poet who has just damned the classics, brings home to us Satan's final downfall in terms of that magnificent old story of Antaeus crushed by the upheld arms of Hercules. Writing *Paradise Regained* must have eased unbearable pressure, for Milton turns with more wholeness of spirit to an Old Testament theme which he presents in an old Greek form too congenial for him to dispense with.

6.

In the intensity of his effort to show reason's supremacy in *Paradise Regained* Milton destroys that delicate balance between reason and passion which enables him in *Comus* and throughout most of *Paradise Lost* to glory untroubled in the God-given senses. Passion, refusing to be exorcised, goes berserk, turning against itself as well as reason. The dislocation is far more violent than in *Comus*, and so the conflict is not held suspended in ambiguity. Denying temptation so savagely only demonstrates its force; thus the real drama of the poem is unpremeditated, incidental and uncontrolled.

With the dread voice past, looking before and after, we wonder all the more at Milton's remarkable grasp of the human predicament in *Paradise Lost* and *Samson Agonistes*, which supplement each other, since the first dwells primarily on temptation and its aftereffects, the second on its aftereffects and redemption. *Samson Agonistes* is no real answer to temptation of the flesh beyond avoiding it, as Samson turns his back on Dalila; but it is not for poetry to give us a positive answer any more than the flat denial of *Paradise Regained*. Fortunately, before he begins to lose artistic detachment toward passion, Milton brilliantly dramatizes temptation in Adam and Eve.

He has a fine though limited dramatic instinct. When not too deeply involved in defending his own truth, he

delights in the actor's, even more the orator's role—
itself a kind of acting. Nowhere is this more apparent
than in the Parliament of Pandemonium, when with
zest and brilliance he assumes in turn five different per-
sonalities. The compromise with truth, which a persuasive orator usually makes, seems not to disturb this wor-
shipper of reason and absolute truth; for he is realist
enough to know, actor enough to enjoy, how much depends, in swaying an audience, on insinuation, timing,
pitch, inflection, gesture. When he comes to Satan's
temptation by happy chance he is again thinking in
oratorical terms:

> As when of old some orator renowned
> In Athens or free Rome, where eloquence
> Flourished, since mute, to some great cause ad-
> dressed,
> Stood in himself collected, while each part,
> Motion, each act won audience ere the tongue,
> Sometimes in height began, as no delay
> Of preface brooking through his zeal of right.
>> P.L., IX, 670–76

Oddly, the very *assumption* of truth, the

> *show* of zeal and love
> To man, and indignation at his wrong

challenges Milton as much as the opportunity through
Satan to voice some stringent objections to the tree of
knowledge.

Postponing his reservations, and we have seen how
serious they are, he is admirably sure of himself in the
Ninth Book. The full burden of Original Sin, the incest
taboo, he has transferred to Satan and Sin. While paying
lip service to the "tree of knowledge," he actually side-

steps the problem of knowledge and makes the sin in Eden a matter of disobedience, human waywardness, and momentary distrust. Taking full advantage of Genesis, he interprets the crisis as deception of Eve rather than Adam; not really deceived, Adam deliberately chooses passion (and death) over reason.[23] Since in his hierarchy Eve is a step below and thus not quite so rational as Adam, he can suspend his conviction that pure reason is unassailable. Temporarily freed from personal involvement, he enjoys for once the necessary combination of sympathy and detachment. He never writes with more profound and subtle penetration than in this encounter between Satan and Eve, and never elsewhere so successfully creates characterizations which are more than projections of himself. He does not make Eve stupid or irrational; rather he grants subtlety and brilliance and favoring circumstances to Satan.

His innate sense of drama is clear from the simplicity and skill with which he sets the stage for Satan's success in a scene which familiarity does not stale. It is noon after a busy morning. Eve is pleasantly tired and hungry. Having earlier won her point with Adam to prove her independence, she is flooded with self-confidence and victory. She is alone in all her beauty and vulnerability. With incomparable skill Milton makes us share every impulse of her senses as well as each twist of thought; and we are equally in Satan's skin and Satan's mind.

First Satan arouses her fatal curiosity by his disguise. The crawling snake appears before her in spectacular

---

[23] This is of course St. Paul's view: "For Adam was formed first, then Eve: and Adam was not deceived, but the woman was deceived and became a transgressor." (I Timothy 2:13–14)

erect coils; the silent snake speaks with human eloquence. At once a stroke of drama and phallic symbol,
his entrance is a love dance from the animal world of
seduction:

> and toward Eve
> Addressed his way, not with indented wave,
> Prone on the ground, as since, but on his rear,
> Circular base of rising folds, that towered
> Fold above fold a surging maze, his head
> Crested aloft, and carbuncle his eyes;
> With burnished neck of verdant gold, erect
> Amidst his circling spires, that on the grass
> Floated redundant: pleasing was his shape,
> And lovely, never since of serpent kind
> Lovelier . . . .
> So varied he, and of his tortuous train
> Curled many a wanton wreath in sight of Eve,
> To lure her eye; she busied heard the sound
> Of rustling leaves, but minded not, as used
> To such disport before her through the field,
>
> . . . .
> He bolder now, uncalled before her stood;
> But as in gaze admiring: Oft he bowed
> His turret crest, and sleek enameled neck,
> Fawning, and licked the ground whereon she trod.
> His gentle dumb expression turned at length
> The eye of Eve to mark his play; he glad
> Of her attention gained, with serpent tongue
> Organic, or impulse of vocal air,
> His fraudulent temptation thus began . . .
>
> *P.L.*, IX, 495 ff.

Since his opening speech skilfully voices her own nar-
cissistic daydreams of surpassing beauty and worth
denied fit audience, no wonder "into the heart of Eve
his words made way." Meanwhile he stimulates the

appetite he knows she feels as noon approaches, for he assaults on every front—all five senses as well as her mind. His story has the intense reality of a dream, and Milton in the telling must have delighted to realize how far in subtlety and richness of implication this metamorphosis surpasses his master Ovid. He was at first, says the Serpent, abject and low like other beasts till he chanced on the goodly tree with its savory fruit growing beyond ordinary reach. To the envy of the other beasts, he climbed and plucked and ate, and lo, not only was his body fed but also that greater hunger of the mind to know all things in heaven and earth. Having snared Eve's attention, he takes sly pleasure in overbaiting the hook:

> But all that fair and good in thy divine
> Semblance, and in thy beauty's heavenly ray
> United I beheld; no fair to thine
> Equivalent or second, which compelled
> Me thus, though importune perhaps, to come
> And gaze, and worship thee of right declared
> Sovereign of creatures, universal dame.
>
> P.L., IX, 602–12

Hypnotized by his tale, she recognizes the excess, but remotely, as we all do when we automatically deprecate while drinking in fulsome flattery.

Once confronted with the Serpent's tree, she of course knows it for what it is and recalls God's command exceeding the law of reason:

> God hath said, "Ye shall not eat
> Thereof, nor shall ye touch it, lest ye die."

This is Satan's biggest hurdle. And this is the supreme oratorical challenge to which Milton rises all the more readily since he has stripped the tree of any meaning beyond arbitrary taboo. Like a cunning Iago incredulous of Othello's naïveté, Satan has already discovered as early as the Fourth Book this one flaw in Eden:

> Knowledge forbidden?
> Suspicious, reasonless. Why should their Lord
> Envy them that? can it be sin to know,
> Can it be death? and do they only stand
> By ignorance, is that their happy state,
> The proof of their obedience and their faith?
> O fair foundation laid whereon to build
> Their ruin! Hence I will excite their minds
> With more desire to know, and to reject
> Envious commands, invented with design
> To keep them low whom knowledge might exalt . . .
>
> *P.L.*, IV, 515–25

Satan is therefore fully prepared with his argument, and kindled by the orator's elation, Milton savors the irony of giving to the Evil One his own convictions about happiness without knowledge, carefully interspersed with obvious tricks and falsehoods so that he will not be hoist by his own petard. Satan constantly draws Eve's attention to his own supposed survival after eating fruit which he has of course never touched; he pretends ignorance and flippant contempt for death, though he knows how nearly overmatched he was in his terrible recognition scene with Death in Hell. For the rest, Milton through the Serpent speaks with genuine conviction:

> Deterred not from achieving what might lead
> To happier life, knowledge of good and evil;
> Of good, how just? of evil, if what is evil
> Be real, *why not known, since easier shunned?*

> God therefore cannot hurt ye, and be just;
> Not just, not God . . . .
> . . . . and wherein lies
> The offense, that man should thus attain to know?
> What can your knowledge hurt him, or this tree
> Impart against his will if all be his?
> Or is it envy, and can envy dwell
> In heavenly breasts? . . .
>
> *P.L.*, IX, 696 ff.

Since his own logic is so much in her favor, Milton probably nowhere else sympathizes more with Eve than here.[24] Of course the occasion is not one for reason, merely for unquestioning obedience; yet all his life Milton himself claimed the privilege of obeying only *reasonable* laws. From what we know of him we suspect that, granted the choice between unconscious good in mindless immortality and a period of wisdom followed by death, Milton would choose the latter. As Eve hesitates, her rationalization of what she is about to do is perilously close to his inner faith:

[24] William Empson in *Some Versions of Pastoral*, 172–80, examines minutely several of Milton's elaborate comparisons as evidence for "the vilification of Eve." Equating Eve with Proserpine and Pandora conveys the traditional idea that Eve, succumbing to the Serpent, tempts Adam and thus looses evil in the world. But Mr. Empson fails to take sufficiently into account both Milton's strong condemnation of Adam when he yields and Milton's uninhibited delight in classical legend in conjunction with Christian belief, even when the joining strikes us as incongruous. There are too many instances of his not altogether apt use of profane matter in Christian passages for us to regard this habit of his as an attack on Eve.

The innate hostility to woman is always present in Milton. Mr. Empson seems to me to exaggerate it in these passages, while failing to recognize the equally strong attraction. It is a question whether this hostility is not primarily directed at sex in man *or* woman, the female merely being the means of revealing what Milton could never quite help considering a basic weakness in man.

For good unknown, sure is not had, or had
And yet unknown, is as not had at all.

But mind is never free from body; temptation is never purely intellectual. This Milton tends to forget occasionally in *Paradise Regained*, but fortunately he accepts it here. Not reason but appetite turns the scale, the appetite man was born to live by—

> raised by the *smell*
> *So savory* of that fruit, which with desire,
> Inclinable now grown *to touch or taste*,
> Solicited *her longing eye*.
>
> P.L., IX, 740–42

To sight, smell, touch, anticipatory taste, is added the seductive lure of Satan's voice glossing over with so much truth one gross lie. Since he conceals his true identity and capitalizes on the deception as proof positive that, far from dying, a snake is exalted by the fruit, Eve's last hold on obedience—her fear of death—is loosened.

Raphael and Adam have put Eve on guard; she should have been wary of any untoward appearance like a talking serpent; yet she is living in a world where new wonders are constantly revealing themselves and where tedium is already a danger. We cannot really blame her. The challenge she meets is fundamental to the human mind, which to become civilized at all beyond a wild or vegetable state has had to break innumerable taboos, always risking failure to distinguish the one true prohibition among so many false, and paying with life. "Whatever thing death be," insinuates Satan, pretending ignorance of his son; and Eve, "How dies the serpent? he hath eaten and lives." Like any rebellious child first taking the name of God in vain, she awaits in fascinated terror and curiosity the swift lightning stroke which does not come. How can she know that death is a continuous but imperceptible process? She would have been safe, but how much less human and less amiable, if like the Lady in *Comus* she had only clung, stubborn and incurious, to faith and obedience.

And so in her rash hour Eve plucks and eats the fruit.

Earth feels the wound. Like Tarquin from Lucrece, the guilty Serpent slinks away, leaving Eve to her intoxicated soliloquy, a poignant mixture of ambition, vanity, jealousy, love. Beneath overweening yet natural desire to "grow mature in knowledge" we discern the smoldering resentment of another's superiority which makes her unconsciously parrot Satan: "for inferior who is free?" Shall she conceal her added stature from Adam? For a time at least she would, were it not for the thought of possible death and with it the chance that she will be replaced by another woman. Her decision is deeply moving:

> Adam shall share with me in bliss or woe:
> So dear I love him, that with him all deaths
> I could endure, without him live no life.
> P.L., IX, 831–33

There is no doubt about her genuine love, yet she is determined more by selfishness and jealousy than by generosity. Not long after, Adam echoes even more fervently this noble sentiment with the same alloy of egoism. Beautiful and romantic as he makes their love for each other, Milton leaves no doubt that it is possessive infatuation. The miracle is that the poet of *Paradise Regained* accepts with such balance of detachment and sympathy this complexity of emotion and portrays it with the assurance of Shakespeare.

7.

Milton's attitude toward woman is complex, or he would not in such closely interlocking sequence produce those tortured love-hate passages in *Paradise Regained*, the harsh self-loathing of Samson, the Tristan-like acceptance of Adam "fondly overcome with female charm." Underneath all these contradictory manifestations is one strong conviction: "Yet beauty, though injurious, hath strange power."

"I cannot praise thy marriage choices, son," old Manoa sadly comments in a line which must have cost Milton pain, for at times he opens in a frenzy of self-torture his deep domestic injury which never heals. Except for beauty's "strange power" the wound would not have gone so deep.

Even during his moments of self-searching, Satan like Saul never really repents any more than Hamlet's uncle truly prays; but at one startling point he is "abstracted . . . from his own evil," for a brief time "stupidly good." This happens when he first comes upon Eve alone in Eden, the opportunity for which he hoped and which he uses to destroy her:

> her heavenly form
> Angelic, but more soft, and feminine,
> Her graceful innocence, her every air
> Or gesture or least action overawed

His malice, and with rapine sweet bereaved
His fierceness of the fierce intent it brought:

. . . .

She fair, divinely fair, fit love for gods,
Not terrible, *though terror be in love*
And beauty . . .

P.L., IX, 457 ff.

This remarkable passage is more revealing, I think, than Milton knew. When an archangel is so swayed, no wonder mere man succumbs.

Terror in love haunts Milton. Belial stresses it again when he describes not sophisticated Cleopatras, but virgins skilled in arts of love by native instinct:

virgin majesty with mild
And sweet allayed, *yet terrible to approach.*
Skilled to retire, and in retiring draw
Hearts after them *tangled in amorous nets*

. . . .

Enerve, and with voluptuous hope dissolve.

P.R., II, 159 ff.

"*Enerve*, and with voluptuous hope *dissolve*" betrays intensity of passion not unexpected in a poet whose imagery reveals sensuousness always trembling into sensuality. Join this susceptibility to extreme pride in independence, and the terror in love is understandable: fear of the loss of control which surrender to love means, fear of orgastic helplessness, fear of himself as well as woman. Dalila literally unmans Samson.

In Milton's sparse gallery of women—the faithless, rather tawdry Dalila; the fiery but impregnable virgin; the frighteningly hostile figure of his first wife ("an image of earth and phlegm")—Eve is the chief exception[25] among the few "not terrible, though terror be in love." His whole treatment of Eve is tender and compassionate, in spite of his latent hostility; if she is essentially a wishful dream, she is at least grounded on a more profound knowledge and tolerance of marriage than Milton usually shows.

Adam's excessive passion is made clear almost from the beginning; he is troubled by it in his long talk with Raphael, who tries to bolster his self-confidence. Perhaps that the story requires this weakness of Adam's as preparation for the climax explains why Milton writes with an untroubled abandon which he never shows elsewhere on this subject, without self-consciousness or inhibition or resentment. And the domestic scene at the opening of the Ninth Book of *Paradise Lost* has simplicity and truth unique in his poetry. Adam is prototype of the uxorious husband, which Milton potentially is, facing for the first time the rude reality of his wife's boredom with love. This reversal of role in itself is a shock to male egoism; usually the husband is first to find domesticity palling. With sad prophecy he warns Eve that Satan may wish to disturb

> Conjugal love, than which perhaps no bliss
> Enjoyed by us excites his envy more;
> Or this, or worse, leave not the faithful side
> That gave thee being, still shades thee and protects.
> The wife, where danger or dishonor lurks,
> Safest and seemliest by her husband stays,
> Who guards her, or with her the worst endures.
>
> *P.L.*, IX, 263–69

[25] There is, of course, that brief vision of "my late espoused saint" in the sonnet to his second wife. Too much Dante-inspired fancy, I think, has played around that adolescent daydream girl of the Seventh Elegy.

After a far more violent quarrel, after Samson dismisses his wife for good, the Chorus propounds this mystery of woman's choice and woman's discontent:

> It is not virtue, wisdom, valor, wit,
> Strength, comeliness of shape, or amplest merit
> That woman's love can win or long inherit;
> But what it is, hard is to say,
> Harder to hit,
> (Which way soever men refer it)
> Much like thy riddle, Samson, in one day
> Or seven, though one should musing sit.
>
> S.A., 1010–17

From his bitter experiences with Timnath's daughter and Dalila, Samson, abandoning any further effort to understand wives, gives his grim solution—the husband's despotic power:

> So shall he least confusion draw
> On his whole life, not swayed
> By female usurpation, nor dismayed.
>
> S.A., 1058–60

There is none of this dismissal of woman as a hopeless enigma in *Paradise Lost*, where Milton not only accepts but sympathizes with Eve. If he enjoys realizing how correctly Adam foresees disaster from their separation he does not show it. Instead he balances against Adam's greater responsibility awareness that overprotection springs from fundamental distrust; he grants to Eve his own conviction that, at whatever cost, virtue to be of value must be exercised:

> If this be our condition, thus to dwell
> In narrow circuit straitened by a foe,
> Subtle or violent, we not endued

Single with like defense, wherever met,
How are we happy, still in fear of harm?

P.L., IX, 322–26

Bemused by the thought that "thy stay, not free, absents thee the more," Adam is outmaneuvered. Already he dreads Eve's discontent. He risks all simply to keep her complaisant.

The quality of Adam's emotion is brought out by a simple but wonderfully effective symbol—the wreath of roses which he weaves for Eve while with a mixture of joy and anxiety he awaits her return; it is to crown "her rural labors" but even more to show her supremacy in his heart. Impatiently he goes forth and meets her at the ill-omened tree. Flustered with guilt and intoxication, she greets him with a spate of words and the pathetic lie that she has eaten the fruit, otherwise despised, for his sake only:

Thus Eve with countenance blithe her story told;
But in her cheek distemper flushing glowed.
On the other side, Adam, soon as he heard
The fatal trespass done by Eve, amazed,
Astonied stood and blank, while horror chill
Ran through his veins, and all his joints relaxed;
From his slack hand the garland wreathed for Eve
Down dropped, and all the faded roses shed.

P.L., IX, 886–93

The bloom leaves the roses as it has already left Eve, and, himself touched by frost, Adam knows he is facing death, "whatever thing death be." His first outcry is the most heart-rending in the poem:

O fairest of creation, last and best
Of all God's works, creature in whom excelled

Whatever can to sight or thought be formed,
Holy, divine, good, amiable, or sweet!
How art thou lost, how on a sudden lost,
Defaced, deflowered, and now to death devote?

P.L., IX, 896–902

Realizing the enormity of their change, for "certain my resolution is to die," he has at this moment no room in his heart for blame.

But purity of motive lasts briefly. He in his turn begins to rationalize, to mingle blame with excuse. All for Love or the World Well Lost—that favorite romantic theme of mankind—has seldom been so simply or so profoundly expressed, for great emotional complexity is subsumed. Far from lessening, it increases the truth and power of this scene to recognize the mixture of motive, the selfishness entangled with sacrifice. Eve's admiration is fervent but double-edged and noncommittal:

"O glorious trial of exceeding love,
Illustrious evidence, example high!
Engaging me to emulate, but short
Of thy perfection, how shall I attain,
. . . . . . whereof good proof
This day affords, declaring thee resolved,
Rather than death or aught than death more dread
Shall separate us, linked in love so dear,
To undergo with me one guilt, one crime,
If any be . . . ."
So saying, she embraced him, and for joy
Tenderly wept, much won that he his love
Had so ennobled . . .

P.L., IX, 961 ff.

Eve is a realist. This demonstration of his love only strengthens her determination that Adam shall join her for good or ill. She does not even consider rising to similar sacrifice by sparing Adam her own guilt. Pressing on him the enticing fruit, she rewards his heroism by death, though death with her.

The irony here is not bitter; it is the alloy giving the metal of heroism the tensile hardness to bear the weight of experience and truth. And when Milton *commends* Eve for this "recompense" he is being seriously moral rather than ironical. Adam puts love of Eve before love of God. The intentional echo of Christ's disinterested offer through love to save mankind underscores the difference between true and questionable self-sacrifice. Eve is afraid to die, Adam to live alone, since "to lose thee were *to lose myself.*" Unlike Eve beset by Satan's subtlest wiles, Adam sins with full knowledge, but with motives so humanly mixed that even moral Milton, who sometimes expects man to rival Christ, while condemning, commends him.

The unhappy effects of the fruit are swiftly apparent in deterioration portrayed with great psychological insight. The love of Adam and Eve becomes lust soon satiated, soon regretted; their harmony dissolves into charge and counter-charge; their innocence gives way to guilt so great that Adam cries out in words reminiscent of Faustus:

> Cover me ye pines,
> Ye cedars, with innumerable boughs
> Hide me, where I may never see them more.
> *P.L.,* IX, 1088–90

More mercurial than Eve, he yearns for suicide, deterred like Hamlet only by fear of what lies beyond. Yet when

Eve suggests two practical methods of suicide, Adam recoils, then recovers his senses and his leadership.

Milton could not grant to the tree knowledge of good, only revelation of evil. By implication this seems to make God guilty of deceit and may be one thing which later troubles him and leads to reformulating the myth, but it does not disturb *Paradise Lost*. By treating the prohibition as a taboo, a test of man's submission to and trust in God, at this climax Milton manages to avoid one issue impelling him to write *Paradise Regained*.

Without unreserved imaginative participation in a basic human drama he could not have achieved this tragic sense of inevitability. Man yields to temptation when he is caught in an archetypical net of circumstance and mixed motivation, from which, being what he is, no amount of faith or foreknowledge can extricate him. Only a pathological egoist or a saint could choose otherwise. The enmeshing of the victims is so beautifully contrived, so close to our experience in each tightening of the thread, that human nature as much as Satan undoes Adam and Eve.

8.

At one point during Adam's disillusion Milton's ambivalent love-hate splits into his characteristic hostility to woman. It is so appropriate to Adam in the circumstances that it does not, as elsewhere, distort the poem:

> Thus it shall befall
> Him who to worth in women overtrusting
> Lets her will rule; restraint she will not brook,
> And left to herself, if evil thence ensue,
> She first his weak indulgence will accuse.
>
> *P.L.*, IX, 1182–86

This complaint becomes a text of *Samson Agonistes;*
but we must remember that we meet Dalila only after
her betrayal.

Nothing in his last poem is so magnificent as the opening books of *Paradise Lost,* or so brilliant and warmly
human as the Ninth Book. To compensate, *Samson
Agonistes* has none of the arid rationalities of *Paradise
Lost,* none of the prolixity and occasional opacity of
Paradise Regained. It is Milton's most perfectly sustained work. Probably he accepts this version of temptation more readily because only disobedience is involved
and because it is double: Samson has a second trial and
on the second triumphantly resists Dalila. Also at the
end Samson gets a chance to redeem himself in what
is actually a form of revenge. Milton by temperament is
closer to the Old than to the New Testament, capable
of great warmth and tenderness and compassion, but
also of exultant wrath—exactly the mixture of emotional extremes which one finds in the Prophets and the
Psalms. The Old Testament heroic tragedy of Samson is
so well adapted to his own temperament and circumstances that the personal and dramatic never interfere
with each other but coincide. There is nothing to block
or divert the strong and bitter flow of passion.

The late point of attack of Greek drama spares him
the need to repeat what he has supremely expressed already in Adam and Eve. When the play opens the temptation to which Samson succumbs, after thrice seeing
through it and resisting, is past, and we find him deep
in remorse and self-loathing, helpless in loss of sight, the
castration of his inner power. His state of mind corre-
sponds to Adam's in the Tenth Book of *Paradise Lost,*

when on the verge of suicide. The Chorus, like an objectification of his inner turmoil, alternately blames and comforts him, as does old Manoa. But Samson, his strength returning as his hair grows again, is beginning to discover a strong core of resistance, which is hardened and tempered by his encounters with Dalila and Harapha of Gath. So far as he can, he cancels his earlier mistake, but there is no suggestion as in *Paradise Regained* that the past can be undone.

Blindness, defeat of high hope, and despair over wasted power, produce in the wonderful opening soliloquy a weariness reminiscent of Hamlet's exhausted fatalism:

> If it be now, 'tis not to come; if it be not to come, it will be now; if it be not now, yet it will come; the readiness is all.
>
> *Hamlet*, V, ii, 233 ff.

But there is a significant difference in Samson's readiness:

> But peace, I must not quarrel with the will
> Of highest dispensation, which herein
> Haply had ends above my reach to know.
>
> S.A., 60–62

This certainty of hidden divine purpose reaches its purest expression in the Christ of *Paradise Regained*, where of course it is untouched by guilt:

> And now by some strong motion I am led
> Into this wilderness, to what intent
> I learn not yet, *perhaps I need not know;*
> *For what concerns my knowledge God reveals.*
>
> P.R., I, 290–93

To the impetuous and imperious, patience comes doubly hard; without faith it is impossible. However extolled throughout the ages, patience strikes the afflicted harshly,

> Unless he feel within
> Some source of consolation from above;
> Secret refreshings, that repair his strength,
> And fainting spirits uphold.
>
> *S.A.*, 663–66

By this time Milton has scornfully cast from him all Calvinism; yet here again lies the beauty of his choice of story. Those who have reservations about Election can hardly object, since Samson *is*, we know, elect of God, and so of course is Milton:

> . . . such as thou hast solemnly elected,
> With gifts and graces eminently adorned
> To some great work, thy glory . . .
>
> *S.A.*, 678-80

This is the faith no despair can shake. This is the way out of the wilderness of the drama's opening mood.

Like a ship in full sail Dalila comes to see once more what feminine wiles can do. She is not so magical a creation as Eve mainly because the story circumscribes her character. She is too glib, full of too many explanations. If she really wanted reconciliation, a subtler woman would never choose this occasion to rub into her husband's wounds reminder of his own mistakes. Samson's original fall would arouse more sympathy and dramatic tension would be heightened if Milton had made her, instead of transparently shallow, subtle like Satan. But his imagination and passion are centered on Samson, who this time does not hesitate:

I led the way; bitter reproach, but true,
I to myself was false ere thou to me,
Such pardon therefore as I give my folly,
Take to thy wicked deed . . .

S.A., 823 ff.

"Such pardon" means precisely none, for Samson does not forgive himself any more than he forgives his wife. Fine as this acceptance of responsibility is, the proud assumption that no one but himself could betray him and the recoil from dependence on woman show extreme male egoism:

How wouldst thou insult
When I must live, *uxorious to thy will*
In perfect thralldom, how again betray me . . .
S.A., 944 ff.

Milton, who in his anxiety to wipe out Adam's fatal uxoriousness unbalances *Paradise Regained,* cannot bring himself to let Samson yield an inch. Dalila leaves, and Milton seizes the occasion for a generalization in which all women become Dalilas as Hamlet makes them Gertrudes. This sweeping condemnation flatly contradicts Adam's beautiful tribute to woman as "last and best of all God's works."

But this is not final. Samson will not let Dalila touch him, for fear he may strike her—and for fear her touch may even now "enerve, and with voluptuous hope dissolve." After she has gone he has a flash of unwonted wistfulness:

Love-quarrels oft in pleasing concord end,
Not wedlock-treachery endangering life.
S.A., 1008–1009

And Milton lets the Chorus rather than Samson reveal that passion while not ruffling the surface still troubles the waters beneath:

> Yet beauty, though injurious, hath strange power,
> *After offense returning, to regain*
> *Love once possessed, nor can be easily*
> *Repulsed, without much inward passion felt*
> *And secret sting of amorous remorse.*
>
> S.A., 1003–1007

Thus in Milton's farewell to the temptation of physical love as a mystery beyond solution there remains to the end a "secret sting of amorous remorse."

Once he has brought himself to part irrevocably with Dalila, Samson is purged of gloom and self-pity and despair. With quiet exultation he awaits the event toward which his being moves. The verse quickens with this lift of spirit into the confidence and zest with which he discomfits Harapha of Gath and accepts the second call to Dagon's feast. As we await with the Chorus and old Manoa the expected catastrophe, we know from the tone and quality of the verse as surely as when a tide changes from ebb to flow that Samson is himself again, with the quiet certainty of a man who knows what is to be done and does it without hesitation and with relief.

Death is a high price to pay for self-reconciliation, but, to the turbulent blood, temptation is present till the end. While Samson by discipline and tenacious faith achieves some calm of mind, only at death is all passion spent.

Critical and Other Works Cited

Allen, D. C. *The Harmonious Vision.* Baltimore, 1954.

Brooks, Cleanth, and John E. Hardy. *Poems of Mr. John Milton.* New York, 1951.

Bush, Douglas. *Mythology and the Renaissance Tradition.* Minneapolis, 1932.

Bush, Douglas. *Paradise Lost in Our Time.* Ithaca, 1945.

Campbell, J. C., and H. M. Robinson. *Skeleton Key to Finnegans Wake.* New York, 1944.

Clark, W. K. Lowther. *Concise Bible Commentary.* New York, 1953.

Empson, William. *Some Versions of Pastoral.* New York, n.d.

Grierson, Sir Herbert J. C. *Milton and Wordsworth.* New York, 1937.

Joyce, James. *Finnegans Wake.* New York, 1939.

Mahood, M. M. *Poetry and Humanism.* New Haven, 1950.

Pope, Elizabeth. *Paradise Regained: The Tradition and the Poem.* Baltimore, 1954.

Reik, Theodor. *Dogma and Compulsion.* New York, 1951.

Stein, Arnold. *Answerable Style.* Minneapolis, 1953.

Waldock, A. J. A. *Paradise Lost and Its Critics.* New York, 1947.

Willey, Basil. *The Seventeenth Century Background.* London, 1934.

Index